Contemporary Approaches to English Studies

Edited by
HILDA SCHIFF

HEINEMANN EDUCATIONAL BOOKS · LONDON
for THE ENGLISH ASSOCIATION

BARNES & NOBLE BOOKS · NEW YORK
(a division of Harper & Row Publishers Inc)

Heinemann Educational Books Ltd
LONDON EDINBURGH MELBOURNE AUCKLAND TORONTO
HONG KONG SINGAPORE KUALA LUMPUR
IBADAN NAIROBI JOHANNESBURG
LUSAKA NEW DELHI KINGSTON

ISBN (U.K) 0 435 18806 2 cased edition
          0 435 18807 0 paperback edition

ISBN (U.S.A.) 0-06-496105-2

set in 11/12 Baskerville

Published in Great Britain by
Heinemann Educational Books Ltd
48 Charles Street, London W1X 8AH
Published in the U.S.A. 1977 by
Harper & Row Publishers, Inc.
Barnes & Noble Import Division

Printed in Great Britain by
Butler & Tanner Ltd, Frome and London

Contents

Introduction

The papers gathered together in the following pages celebrate an occasion and mark a new departure. The occasion was the first Symposium ever to be held by the English Association, initiated with the intention of expanding the Association's activities and developing its involvement in the vast spectrum of interests centred on a concern for English literature and its language.

It must be explained at the outset that this volume does not pretend to offer a conspectus of the range of activity now operative within the field of English studies. Such a survey would lie outside the scope of a single publication and would be incidental to our purpose. What we offer the reader here is a coherent set of current approaches to English studies, extending from the traditional to the emergent.

Each approach presented in these pages is the representative expression of a critic who is in a position of considerable influence today. These critics, working at the frontiers of their subject and presenting widely divergent standpoints, help us both to measure the astonishing distance that English as a field of study has travelled in this century, and to chart some courses that it is likely to take in the future.

For, as those involved in the study and teaching of English literature well know, little more than fifty years ago English as a subject in the academic sense had barely begun. Today English might be claimed as one of the most popular of subjects amongst students, and its specializations as remarkably numerous. While this rapid growth has its puzzling aspects, in part we can attribute it quite simply to the growth of populations in general and to their greatly extended literacy. Moreover, with the decline of formerly central subjects such as classics and theology, the study of literature has seemed to offer the student of it some alternative enlightenment concerning the nature of the human condition, and it has also appeared to act as a guide to individual and social values in an ever more estranging universe. While today many people question the validity and effectiveness of this position which stems from

Matthew Arnold's teaching, nevertheless all around us we continue to witness the assured popularity of English literature as a subject. This is all the more noteworthy, and perhaps significant, in the light of the scarcity of related vocational opportunities awaiting English graduates.

This situation is in marked contrast to that which obtained in 1906 when the English Association was first founded to promote the study of English literature and its language.[1] Then the subject 'English' was in its infancy and was regarded as very *infra dig.* both intellectually and socially. Throughout the nineteenth century English had been taught mainly in schools for less privileged children and in the Dissenting Academies. Not until the end of the century was it introduced into English universities as part of degree work, and then only into London and the provincial universities, whose students were largely working- and middle-class. Usually the syllabus ended prior to Tennyson and Browning, and Anglo-Saxon, Gothic, and Middle English were obligatory joint accomplishments, intended, by some at least, to 'stiffen up' the subject. In 1896 and 1919 respectively, after much in-fighting, Oxford and Cambridge followed suit. However, in these august centres, as elsewhere, English as a subject was for long thought to be a poor thing, a view which was lent what appeared to be self-evident corroboration by the fact that the majority of students reading English were women. For men students, classics still retained a monopoly of intellectual and social *cachet* until well into the later 1930s, English being regarded as a soft option' for them.

In view of this state of affairs it is quite remarkable that the subject of English has developed to the extent it has, a fact which reflects ironically upon a whole host of earlier social, sexual and pedagogic preconceptions. However, while English *scholarship* has advanced so rapidly, the real theoretical backwardness of English studies as compared with other disciplines may be attributable to those early historical factors alluded to above. For even today, when so many able men and women drawn to English studies bring to it an admirable and indispens-

---

1. It was founded by two schoolmasters, E. S. Valentine and G. E. S. Coxhead, and took the initiative in promoting the Board of Education Report of 1921 concerning the teaching of English, to which many eminent scholars gave evidence, including Sir Walter Raleigh who greatly inspired the English School in Oxford in its early days. See *The Origins and History of the English Association*, by Nowell Smith, 1942.

able sensitivity towards literature and its language, few are prepared to look analytically at the modes of operation whereby they pursue their own work. And it is precisely at this juncture that we can discern an important historical watershed between the establishment, extension, and consolidation of English studies, and the possible future development of English as a systematic subject, that is, as a field of knowledge *about* literary works, in which knowledge can be not only augmented but also advanced.

For what is happening at last on the frontiers of English studies is that, as in other humane disciplines that have bothered to look outwards (notably linguistics or anthropology), we are now asking questions about what we are doing and the way we are doing it with some rudimentary understanding that, as Coleridge pointed out long before Wittgenstein, the world is half composed of what we observe and half of what we create by the manner *in which* we perceive.[2] Whether it happens to be to our taste or not, the transformation that is overtaking us inside the field of English is, and must be, one of methodological awareness if progress is to be made.

Many readers will be understandably sceptical about what good such procedural analyses will do, and will aver that now as ever the essential business of criticism is to interpret literary texts and to evaluate them. They will claim that traditionally the study of literature has been empirical, and that to analyse and theorize about our work is not only useless but might lead us to legislate, and that to legislate is inevitably to constrict those who create and those who appraise those creations. Very few would disagree with the last element of such an argument; yet it is equally clear that in attempting to extend a field of study, no innovator can be expected to predict precisely what benefits may result from the pursuit of disinterested curiosity. And surely where a subject makes no room for 'useless' enquiries it is likely to become petrified.

Some of the questions we need to ask then are these. In studying literature, what *is* it we are doing? What are our assumptions concerning the objects of our inquiries and the modes of our procedures, and are they justifiable and increasingly fruit-

---

2. For instance, we may come to learn something about our ordinary account of art by noting that Einstein showed that gravitation, a condition most natural to us, distorted light rays, that is, the medium by means of which we observe.

ful, or merely repetitive in their results? Further, what would it *mean* to make advances in our subject? We know very little about the answers to these questions. What we do know is that one way of looking for answers is to examine closely procedures in other fields of knowledge where progress has indubitably occurred. We can then consider in what respects our own field compares and contrasts with theirs.

We know for instance that work in any branch of 'hard' knowledge generally falls into one of two categories, inductive and deductive. The first method which proceeds from the particular to the general is often based on intuitive work, a 'blind' accumulation and description of almost random data, which eventually, when collated, appears as an explanatory configuration of wide applicability. Alternatively, deductive work, which proceeds from a coherently formulated framework from the outset, goes on to examine a wide spectrum of related data as to their support of the initial explanatory hypothesis. If the hypothesis and the data do not 'fit', and the accuracy of the data has been re-examined, the hypothesis is either abandoned in favour of a new formulation, or it is refined and adjusted in the light of detailed observation. Whether investigation is conducted on an inductive or deductive basis, throughout, it proceeds on the assumption that to know about the world is to know about the system by which it functions. In such a context, the words 'to know', or 'to understand', by definition, mean to comprehend a system of organization which is true for all men until it is superseded by an alternative explanatory system.

What counts as progress within such a field is, on the one hand, either the creation of a new and more comprehensive explanatory hypothesis of greater simplicity than that which obtained before, and which is substantiated by the given body of facts it purports to explain. Or, on the other hand, progress takes place when a given explanatory framework becomes so refined as a consequence of its adjustment to detailed observation, as to result in a very high degree of sophistication and precision, sometimes leading to a practical application. Thus the outcome may be measured in terms of either wider and sharper understanding, or it may be manifest in practical innovations.

The purposes of methodological analysis are: to eliminate

distortions arising from errors of logic, or hidden bias, contained within a particular problem-setting; to check the design and conduct of experiments; and to delineate projects that are proper to the nature of the subject itself. We may liken this task to that of a painter who, before commencing his work, examines his brushes and oils, not only for their quality and cleanliness, but also with a view to considering in what ways they necessarily determine what he can express with them, and by what other means he can overcome their limitations and distortions. The development of new techniques in art have often generated new forms of perception, as is well known.

Can a closer examination of such models help us in English studies? It has been argued[3] that because human affairs, which are the material of literary works, are by their nature so intractable, such systematic models as referred to above are totally inappropriate in seeking to extend our field of study. But surely, as students of literature, we are concerned not with the material of human affairs directly, but with literary *works*, however uncertain the relationship between these two may be. And even while the same dense, random, and 'given' nature of things may be ascribed to art as to life, would it not help us to devise a new and more progressive mode of inquiry by clarifying in what specific respects other models do *not* apply? In delineating our differences we may well succeed in defining our own essential nature, and thus discovering a way forward.

For in English studies today our methods are both inductive and deductive to this extent. Given a handful of more or less rational criteria, such as some recourse to evidence to support an interpretation, or the principle of consistency in presenting an argument, any critic's 'reading' of a text does in fact offer a quasi-systematic explanatory framework for it which either 'emerges' as a result of a description of the separate elements of a work (the data), or which the details of the work are called upon to corroborate. Where we then proceed to 'soften' is in going on to accredit equal weight, and thus authority, to rival 'readings' (or we might call them explanatory accounts), and for no better reason than that the symbols of art legitimately

3. See A. J. Ayer, *Man as a Subject for Science*, 1964, and I. Berlin, 'The Concept of Scientific History , in *Generalization in Historical Writing*, ed. Riasanovsky and Riznik. U.S A., 1963.

evoke a multiplicity of responses, a point which no one would wish to challenge. Yet responses are not interpretations, nor is an 'appreciation' however sensitive, a fully articulated and logically coherent appraisal which could count as indubitable knowledge about a given literary work.

As teachers of English well know, students who have not yet been brainwashed continually ask, whether explicitly or implicitly, how it is possible to 'prove' that *King Lear* or *Anna Karenina* are great literary works. How do we respond to this question? We proceed to display our personal appreciation for these works, using rhetorical devices calculated to persuade them that their question is illegitimate. As a result, if our students' taste does not correspond to our own, we feebly conclude that literature is 'obviously not their subject'. Yet all of us do feel, and sometimes think, that there are, or must be, hard 'facts' about these works, as there are hard facts about the Parthenon, or even the more apparently intangible qualities of a Mozart aria. Once apprised of these 'facts', every English teacher should be able to say: these are the reasons why this literary work is great, and any person not totally brutalized can appreciate its greatness, even though it may well be that I/you/someone else may not *like* the work, that is, it may not be to their taste. We ought to be in a position to say: here are the 'facts' and this is the most fully articulated model or system we have devised to date for explaining their organization and function: master it.

Sadly, however, in English studies we remain by and large at a stage where we are still extremely uncertain of what we mean when we talk even of 'the facts' in connection with literary works. My belief is that we do not know more precisely than we do, not because the problem is so overwhelmingly difficult, but simply because we do not spend long enough asking the questions, and looking further afield with regard to how to set these questions up.

What *is* it that we do when we study literature? Do we live at second hand? Do we merely observe, or reconstitute, or rearrange objects, persons, events, and feelings *through* language, or by means of language, into what we like to call shape, in some way yet exceedingly shadowy to our understanding? And what relation does this so-called shape bear to what is 'really' there before us: could it be merely black marks on the page?

Many critics have spoken illuminatingly of literary works that are undoubtedly of great importance to us: what is it exactly that they have done for us, and exactly how? Have they reconstructed an experience of an experience? Have they merely analysed in language an autonomous language act? What *is* it to speak prose, to write verse, to engage in criticism? Is there any precise meaning to the expression 'the development of literary discrimination' beyond a compilation of likes and dislikes? We might do well in English studies to look into this mirror with the assistance of a Chomsky or Levi-Strauss of our own could we but find one. Few of us however have thought of making room enough for even a false messiah.

· I have seen it as my function as editor to formulate such questions for the reader and to point out that the following papers are situated within a context that takes account of their existence. Most of the writers whose work now follows need no introduction to their readers throughout the English-speaking world. Jointly their attitudes span the watershed in the vast territory of English studies to which I previously alluded. Their approaches range from that of biographical criticism of the more traditional kind, through Marxist criticism, to Structuralist criticism. Each author is acutely conscious of the work of others not only within his own but also in other specializations. Many important questions are raised, sometimes echoing each other, and sometimes resolved in conflicting ways. The short further reading list appended to each contribution is intended to aid the reader in following up these issues.

What is common to all the contributors to this volume, and what unites them, is a sense of the relevance of their ongoing debate to the future development of the subject of English. Above all, they share with the editor the determination to look out beyond the horizons of their own specializations, where we may find that the knowledge of others will eventually succeed in revolutionizing our own.

Why English?

GEORGE STEINER

It is certainly difficult, and almost certainly foolhardy, to say anything about the condition of a language as a whole. The elements of the case are too numerous and intricate. It is, moreover, doubly difficult to do so when speaking from within the particular language. In this situation one is attempting to escape from one's own skin or shadow, to discover a privileged locale outside the fabric of one's own articulate identity. But there is no such neutral ground, and it is by acting as if there were that current theories of formal or universal linguistics show their arbitrariness.

Thus to speak of, and to, the condition of English in English is to be enmeshed inside the vital realities which one is seeking to objectify, and which one is trying to see from a certain clarifying distance. But to speak of this condition in another tongue would be to forfeit an essential immediacy and authority of felt being. The resulting dilemma, the circularity, are unavoidable. One does one's best, piecemeal, and with the sensation of getting important perspectives just a bit out of focus because one is standing too close, and because they matter too greatly.

This discomfort, and the urgency of concern and involvement from which it springs, are, I think, justified. For to address ourselves to the present condition of English is not to advance a merely technical, professional argument, though a good deal of the pertinent evidence will indeed be of a technical and professional sort. It is to attempt to say something about nothing less than the social, political and psychological realities of British life and feeling at this time. It is to suggest that Carlyle's celebrated tag 'the condition of England question' will, in notable respects at least, and with little restriction of its purposed breadth of implication, translate into a 'condition of English question'.

This is a large claim. It has behind it a theory, or to be more modest, a deliberate, rationally structured intuition, about the intimate, mutually-informing connections between human speech and human society, between individual discourse and political substance. It is a claim which posits a strong image or metaphor of language as an organic-social aggregate whose condition both reflects and helps to determine the fortunes of the society in which it is spoken. By no means all historians, sociologists or even linguists would accept this model of a determining relation. But if we keep in mind that what we are using is only a working hypothesis, and that the evidence cannot be made finally systematic, the evidence as we have it does suggest that the condition of language and of society constitutes an interactive whole. The French conservative thinker, de Maistre, put forward this idea in the early nineteenth century. Karl Kraus, the Viennese satirist and political visionary, devoted a lifetime to demonstrating the reciprocities of linguistic and social phenomena—how the politics of language is the language of politics—in the German-speaking world before, during and after the catastrophe of 1914. In our own syllabus the most impressive statements of this perspective are those of George Orwell.

I am persuaded that the implicit conjunction is valid. To consider the present state of the English language, even in a tentative, cursory way, is to consider the shaping forces in contemporary British society and some of the crucial modes in which that society views itself and its relations to the outside world.

The first, most obvious point to make is that the linguistic centre of English has shifted. This is so demographically. Great Britain now makes up only a small portion of the English-speaking totality. 'Totality', furthermore, is quite the wrong word. The actual situation is one of nearly incommensurable variety and flux. Any map of 'world-English' today, even without being either exhaustive or minutely detailed, would have to include the forms of the language as spoken in many areas of East, West and South Africa, in India, in Ceylon, and in United States' possessions or spheres of presence in the Pacific. It would have to list Canadian English, the speech of Australia, that of New Zealand, and above all, of course, the manifold shades of American parlance. Yet although such a catalogue would comprise hundreds of millions of English speakers whose idiolects and communal usage would vary all the way from West Indian speech to Texan, or from the cadences of Bengal to those of New South Wales and the Yukon, it would be very far from complete.

English is now disseminated across much of the planet. It is the explicitly taught second language for large sections of the Soviet Union, China, Japan, Scandinavia or the Netherlands. It has become (overlooking the irony of the phrase) the *lingua franca* of an age of technology, material growth and consumer demand. It is not Esperanto or any other interlingual which has come anywhere close to the needs and programmes of a universal medium of communication and of commercial and scientific consensus. It is English, though in a form or variety of forms, distant from the mother-tongue.

But this shift of the linguistic centre involves far more than statistics. It does look as if the principal energies of the English language, as if its genius for acquisition, for innovation, for metaphoric response, had also moved away from England. In saying this, I am certainly on questionable ground. How does one measure the 'energies' of a language? Are 'richness', 'resilience', 'acquisitiveness' when applied to language anything more than impressionistic similes? Obviously, we are not here in the domain of the exact, and quantification, even on a fairly rough and ready scale, is difficult. But studies of the expansion or contraction of vocabulary, of grammatical resource, or acquiescence in or resistance to new lexical and semantic elements can be made, and even if the results remain approximate, significant tendencies can be discerned.

In respect of lexical enrichment and phonetic elaboration, of syntactic flexibility and of sheer 'drive'—that pulsing pressure of the spoken word which is at once the most difficult to measure yet also the most palpable quality in the speech habits of a community—the 'variant-English' of the Caribbean, of certain West African societies, of Australia makes much of metropolitan usage sound grey and worn.

This is pre-eminently true of American English. Under the pressure of minority tongues, notably Spanish and Yiddish, under the compulsion of a stress and density of physical, social, emotional experience unmatched, perhaps, in any other contemporary political system, American English (and in this case too one would have to look at the plurality of local modes) has entered on an Elizabethan phase. At its vernacular and even argotic best, spoken, sung, written American displays that appetite for neologism, that capacity to domesticate imports from foreign tongues and from the special languages of the sciences, of music, of sports, that enchantment with and by metaphor, that spendthrift joy in the feel and multiplicity of words and syntactic turns which energized the English English of the sixteenth and seventeenth centuries. Hence the magnetism, the dynamics of diffusion which, via film and pop lyrics, via television and the media of mass consumption, have made of American speech the dialect of acquisitive dreams and of the young the world over. So far as it is indeed the world-language, English is, essentially, American English.

Literature at once embodies and generates such underlying mutations of linguistic vitality. If one says this, one is compelled to name names and to ascribe orders of magnitude. There are those who claim that it is 'vulgar' to do so. This is unctuous nonsense. The reader, the teacher, the critic, the literary historian will always urge discriminations. Aristotle did so when he termed Euripides 'the most tragic of dramatists'; Dr Johnson founded his confident canon of values on a contrastive ordering of individual writers; T. S. Eliot saw certain masters as dividing the world between them. Today too it is the critic's job of work not to assign handicaps in some imaginary Derby—the relation of reader to writer will always, where it is genuine, be one of private valuation, of needs and echoes profoundly personal, and contemptuous, if need be, of public hierarchies—but to map distinctions between central presences and the peripheral, between the kind of vision and linguistic performance which alters the landscape of sensibility and that which only repeats, varies or adorns. If he does so, if he honestly proposes to identify 'touchstones' (Matthew Arnold's term for the necessary ordering of significance), the critic, the committed reader of modern letters in the English language, will find himself less and less drawn to home ground.

He will not, for example, discover much in the British setting to compare with the visionary compass of the novels of Patrick White or with the probing concentration of Nadine Gordimer. He will know that little in British polemics, social argument and reportage, certainly after Orwell, is of a class with the craft of Norman Mailer or James Baldwin. He will be aware that the current American novel, reaching as it does from the often arcane, narcissistic conceits of Nabokov and John Updike to the classic humanism of Saul Bellow and the experiments, *in extremis*, of Thomas Pynchon or Robert Coover, now represents the richest, most complex interplay of intelligence and of style in the language. He will bridle at the wilful prolixity and, indeed, self-indulgence of numerous elements in Pynchon's novel, *Gravity's Rainbow*, but acknowledge at the same time that he is in the presence of the kind of imaginative risk, of narrative genius, of seriousness on the political, philosophic level almost entirely lacking from the home scene. Robert Pirsig's *Zen and the Art of Motorcycle Maintenance* tells us that types of allegory as deliberate as Spenser's are operative still, and that the allegorical springs characteristic of classic American fiction, in Hawthorne and Melville, are fiercely alive. As one French critic has put it, the English language, so far as it finds realization in literature, *est à l'heure du roman américain*.

Being simultaneously so pivotal to a culture and so private, poetry is the most elusive of literary genres to categorize. There are very distinguished poets at work in Britain. But again it would be myopic to deny the exemplary impetus of the American achievement, from the writings of Eliot, Pound and Wallace Stevens, to those of Lowell, Berryman, Plath and Ammons. It is the American voice which has forced British poetry after Hardy to define itself either by allegiance or by denial. W. H. Auden's mid-Atlantic stance was, as it were, the emblem of the new relation.

Moreover, if he is being serious about the general field of imaginative force, the reader, the literary critic, the historian of literature, will know full well that this displacement of magnitude dates back to the turn of the century at least. Shaw, Yeats, Joyce, Beckett are voices out of Ireland. Henry James, T. S. Eliot, Ezra Pound, Wallace Stevens, Ernest Hemingway, William Faulkner are writers utterly rooted in American ground, whatever the choices or refusals of exile in the individual instance. The shaping crises and responses of literature in the English language in what is called 'modernism' or, quite simply, twentieth-century writing, have come from outside. There are major exceptions, of course: in the best of D. H. Lawrence's fiction (and one must stress the need for selection), in the poetry and prose of Thomas Hardy, an achievement whose full educative agency has yet to be felt, in the idiosyncratic and primarily atavistic prodigality of John Cowper Powys, in the work of Orwell. But these are, or from our present focus seem to be, exceptions. The major currents, often muddied and tumultuous, flow elsewhere.

But it is not individual names that matter, however fascinating or even representative, nor even 'schools' and 'movements', such rubrics being so often contrived after the fact. Certainly one is bound to get this or that crucial feature of the landscape blurred (which is no reason to stop: only the trimmer is afraid of mistaking his passions). What matters is the attempt, vulnerable, provocative as it is, to grasp underlying causes and consequences. What matters most is to try to ask the right questions, questions central and supple enough so that even an inaccurate or fragmentary answer will give rise to collaborative disagreement and to better questions.

What lies behind the relative decline, if it is that, in the vigour, the adaptive reflexes, in the capacities to generate personal and social coherence and audacity of perception, in English as it is spoken and written in Great Britain? Is it possible, is it responsible to try to relate the lexical, grammatical, semantic status of the Vulgate, so far as this status can be viewed as a whole (a large proviso), to that of the literature, to that of social and political attitudes and conflicts in Britain between and after two world wars?

The very phrasing of the question seems to invite a plausible reply. Periods of oral and written eloquence, of semantic elaboration, of lexical expansion and literary zest often coincide with periods of political ascendancy. This has been so of Periclean Athens, of Augustan Rome, of Elizabethan and Victorian England, of the Spanish 'golden century', of the France of Louis XIV. The rapid evolution of American fiction, poetry and popular diction to a dominant place in the overall structure of the English language has paralleled the expansion of American material power and influence in this century. Conversely, Spanish literature declined drastically after the exhaustion of the Spanish imperial system. By analogy it could well be argued that certain features of diminution in the liveliness and imaginative authority of British speech and writing are a natural correlative of the larger changes in Great Britain's status and influence. Such diminution would reflect and, as it were, 'encode' the economic and political decline which, it appears, now press upon us with graphic discomfort. Language and literature also follow the flag, and when the latter goes to half-mast certain reductions ensue.

This argument holds out great temptations on grounds of intuitive credibility, of logic, of historical precedent. It incarnates Orwell's conviction, or that of Leavis, that the decayed state of the English language is directly concomitant with that of a nerveless and vulgarized political society. Yet it is just because such a correlation is so tempting that it must be treated with extreme caution. There have been cases—Byzantium, Alexandria, the flowering of German literature in the late eighteenth and early nineteenth centuries—in which manifest political weakness and even national dislocation have coincided with a high and energetic literary output. The interactions between society and speech, between a political climate and the state of the arts, are doubtless organic and reciprocally formative. But they are of so inward and complicated an order, the causal factors are so difficult to isolate, the quantum jumps of individual talent or individual frustration so impossible to predict (a Mozart in episcopal Salzburg!), that generalizations are almost futile.

It is conceivable, certainly, that the current condition of spoken and written English in Britain, in comparison with its own past and with other modes of the language in use all over the globe, does reflect or accord with the decline in the fortunes of the United Kingdom. It is conceivable that the contrasts which impress one as between Elizabethan, Augustan, and Victorian linguistic energies and those apparent today can be related to a more general reduction of material and psychological confidence or creativity. But this hypothesis is bound to remain vague and, quite possibly, unconvincing. We simply do not have sufficient evidence, nor in fact any very clear picture of the psychological and social connections which may be involved.

However, whether or not we understand the underlying causes and mechanisms which may relate the depressed state of the language to that of the body politic, certain effects are worth identifying. At the self-conscious, publicly articulate end of the scale, the approved note today is one of more or less acid parsimony. Rhetoric is out, eloquence is suspect, copiousness of word and grammatical ornament or elaboration are distasteful. The favoured register is one of deflation, of ironic undercutting (a move profoundly different from the Victorian trope of understatement, based as it was on supreme implicit confidence). A levelling acerbity animates or, rather, dehydrates our speech. It is very nearly as if the wealth of the language had been expended over lavish centuries. The current strategy is one of hoarding and small coin (long before Lévi-Strauss, Swift taught us how subtly intimate are the reciprocities between loquacity and liquidity, between speech and coin in the circulatory system of a society).

Representative works in recent English literature illustrate this situation. The poetry of Geoffrey Hill, the novels of Ivy Compton-Burnett, the plays of Harold Pinter exhibit virtuosities of thrift and reduction. Concomitantly the great spenders—John Cowper Powys, David Jones, Lawrence Durrell—are set aside. The prevailing aesthetic is one of compaction and sparsity. As little skin as possible is shown to the wind. We are confronted with a practice of minimalism comparable to the minimalist techniques in certain modern schools of painting and of music. A grey chill has almost become the testimonial of honesty.

This stance, albeit levelling and punitive in its effects, nevertheless embodies a highly sophisticated notion of linguistic possibility. Pinter's laconic, monosyllabic barbs derive their pressure, their paradoxical suggestion of ceremony, from riches discarded or spurned, but once felt. At the lower end of the scale more massive, unsettling phenomena are current. We did not need the Bullock Report to tell us of the disastrous range of sub- and semi-literacies which now harass the schoolteacher and which may bring to the edge of collapse the entire ideal of comprehensive and universal education. We need only pay attention to the usage around us to experience a drastic sense of impoverishment, brutalization and monosyllabic vandalism. Mass speech in Britain today is evidence, at once aggressive and poignant, of radical breaks and devaluations in the fabric of community (a term, a concept, inseparable from the cognate words 'communication' and 'communion'). The monosyllabic obscenity interposed with indifferent frequency between the speaker and his world, or spat out in hostility, is all too expressive of fundamental monotonies and frustrations, and of abandonments of shared discourse. Such abandonments corrode and even destroy the structure of political coherence even as autism corrodes and destroys the identity of the child.

You will say that this has always been more or less the case, that there is in our imaginings of a lost articulateness and cultivation of feeling an element of strategic nostalgia, of élitist condescension. When was popular speech not brutal and reductive of linguistic means? This may indeed be so (evidence is hard to come by). But there are today new and threatening factors. Even where it carried the burden of deprivation and political impotence, British lower-class speech often embodied genuine autonomies, genuine strengths of graphic imagining. Their source might be that of dialect, region or liturgy. Immediacies and inheritances of religious idiom or reference ran like a vivid thread through the monotone of daily jargon. These strengths, moreover, were sustained by techniques of oral knowledge and transmission, by routines, often astonishingly comprehensive and flexible of remembrance. Now the flood-tides of the lowest common denominator as they race outward from the mass media and metropolitan emporia of entertainment are cutting the old roots. The Vulgate is being swamped by the vulgar. Dialect and specificity of sentiment are being eroded and replaced by the thin, uniform wash of the media-code (voices under the hair-dryer).

Secondly, there is the problem of 'Americanization' or, one might almost say, of 'pidginization'. The flood of 'American English', or, to be precise, of a kind of 'pseudo-American pop-English' which passed over Great Britain in the post-war era, reflects far more than the realities of the American military-economic presence in the land—though these realities have obviously counted for much. It reflects a much more crucial and complex dislocation, perhaps one ought to say re-location, of consciousness. Whether justified or not, American English, certainly in the period from the 1920s to the mid-60s brought with it, literally enacted, a promise of material happiness. All over the earth, but especially in Britain, where the externals of the language were shared, the less privileged, the young, the newly enfranchised (and here the role of feminine consciousness and assertion is important) found in the American idiom an exhilarating vision of social progress, sexual fulfilment and psychological liberation. Pulsing outward via television, the films, popular music and the style of the mass-circulation newspapers and magazines, American speech seemed to carry with it not just the actual dishwasher, home-permanent, bowling alley and tv-dinner, but a whole mythology or contract of egalitarian change. In a way which is difficult to define yet palpable, American speech-habits, popular locutions, neologisms, incarnate a constant futurity, a semantic of material perfectibility.

This semantic has radically penetrated British mass-specch. But given the economic inhibitions, the political atrophies and class tensions in the actual British milieu, the import did not generate those compensating virtues of lyric gusto, innovation and acquisitive suppleness which, as we have noted, characterize the authentic American version. In other words 'American English' as it is used or mimed in this country is a packaged, adulterated brand, as is the meat patty which, with a betraying mixture of bravado and embarrassment, proclaims itself a hamburger.

The third and most important change is the transfer of political-economic powers to a new, much wider social spectrum. It may well be the case that literacy and a concordant sense of the importance of the language were always a possession of the few; but these few governed the community and spoke to the world at large as well as to themselves as if they were the natural, justified representatives of the many, indeed of the whole. Their ideals, their criteria of articulateness, stylized and insulated as they may have been, had the force of the obvious. This is no longer so. Mass education, the redistribution of wealth, trade-union and populist claims to a just, perhaps commanding, share of the rights and rewards provided by the social system, are reshaping Britain. The question of the language in which these claims are urged or resisted, the question of the establishment of a common ground for discourse in a new and drastically antagonistic order of social priorities, is assuming unprecedented importance. How shall we understand one another's values, one another's conventions of reference clearly enough in order to disagree creatively? How shall we keep communication alive to the needs of community? Here again, the 'condition of England question' is, in one substantive sense, a 'condition of English question'.

Let me summarize. English is today the principal world-language. On present evidence its spread will continue. The scientific-technological and the commercial lifelines of our age are knit by the use of English as those of the Roman imperial era and its aftermath were by the use of Latin. This centrifugal movement has led to the development of a whole gamut of lexical, syntactic and semantic forms more or less deviant from the metropolitan norm. It has led also to displacements in the centres of linguistic vitality, most notably to the United States. So far as literature may be seen as an index of language-energy, one finds that a significant portion of the writing being produced not only in American English, but also in African, Australian, Anglo-Irish or West Indian idioms, displays an inventive *élan*, an exploratory delight in linguistic resources, a sheer scope largely absent from the British scene. But the process is also one of feedback. Through immigration, travel, import, and the immense influence of the mass media—in which the component of 'Americanism' and of American styles of sensibility is largely dominant—the forms of English spoken and written overseas return to the mother tongue. They press on British usage and feeling in many and complex ways. At the elevated end of the scale this pressure is often deplored and resisted (Mr Amis's barrage at the 'hateful' American novel, Dr Leavis's animadversions on the corruption of ancient purities through transatlantic shoddiness). Thus the austerities, the deflationary thrift which characterize so much of the prevailing anti-rhetoric in educated British diction and literature today can be understood both as a symptom of a generally reduced national status and as a more or less conscious act of opposition to the profligate grossness and noise-levels of the American voice.

At the very same moment, however, it is just this voice, or congerie of voices, which have penetrated and reshaped much of popular parlance and sentiment in this country. Shot through as they are with multiple shadings of partial or subliteracy and with a bitter resentment of traditional speech-norms and the political power-relations which these speech-norms embodied, popular parlance is now taking on an unprecedented social importance. It is not only, as Leavis or Raymond Williams have shown, that the old stabilities and local spontaneities are eroded. It is that the Newspeak of the masses, of the partial literate, is demanding to be heard at every level of political decision. As a result, the student and teacher of English finds himself involved in a linguistic-social fabric of hitherto unknown variousness and consequence. The tongue in which he conducts his essential task of self-realization and transmission is under unprecedented stress from without as well as from within. It is, therefore, no exaggeration to say that the matter of teaching, of speaking, of writing English in Britain now and tomorrow does bear directly on the matter of the identity and future shape of the society as a whole.

What then (to borrow the most famous of modern interrogatives) shall we do?

The requisite vision is, I believe, twofold, and its two principal directions and motions of spirit are in some contradiction. First, there is the obligation, the opportunity to make our sense of the history of the English language and of its literatures more comprehensive, more responsive to the great tributaries from outside. This is to see the evolution of English towards world currency as inseparable from its native genius and as related to every stage of its linguistic development. At the level of responsive reading this view entails the realization, for example, that the tradition of meditative argument and symbolic narrative active in Spenser, Milton and Wordsworth continues in, and is modified by, the practice of Wallace Stevens. It involves the recognition, soon felt to be self-evident, that the development of social-political theatre in the English language includes not only the home product (at present singularly meagre), but also the achievements of Sean O'Casey, Arthur Miller and Athol Fugard. The teacher and analyst of the language must do what he can to register the interplay between the native stock and the deepening pressures, both of intrusion and of dissemination or even dissipation, which come from the new centres of English overseas and from the modulation of English into a sort of international pidgin. He will have to act simultaneously as custodian and welcomer. But these are relatively straightforward and bracing challenges.

What is far more difficult, and charged with political shrapnel, is the task, the most urgent task, of developing genuine literacies and a language-consensus in the rapidly-changing British community. The former, élite criteria of accent, of articulacy, of assumed reference and unforced recognition—Biblical, classical, historical-literary—helped to create a régime unsurpassed, perhaps, in the arts of government, of tolerant dissent and of self-recruitment. Those who 'spake the tongue that Shakespeare spake', or at least implied that it was current to their memories and comprehension, formed a community of echo with immediate implications in terms of shared values. No other modern political community for so long sustained a level of discourse at once conservative—reference, citation are the very instruments of a conservative possibility—and exploratory of rational change.

But as we all know, these conventions and the hierarchies of esteem and actual power which they embodied are now quickly passing away. No artifice of isolation from an Americanized or populist world, no refuge in nostalgic visions of wheelwrights' shops or Arnoldian groves, will restore the old dispensation. The politics of British existence are now crucially inwoven with the habits of definition, of communication, of desire and conflict as they are enacted in the language of the sixteen-year-old school-leaver. Given this fact, the teacher of English, particularly in the comprehensive and secondary-modern school, comes as close as anyone can to being the architect of a potential consensus, of a shared language-field in which social disagreements and generational resentments erupt neither into violence nor into silence (that other mask of violence). Ways must be found—and in this context necessity must be allowed to overlap with utopia—of giving an evolving mass-society a stake in literacy, of bringing to those who have never known them, or known them only at the distance of derision, some elements at least of the immeasurable strength of the language, a strength at once individual and collective, and some elements at least of its history and of its letters.

To an extent which the social historian has had to take almost for granted, the great majority of men and women in this country, now and in the past, have been all but excluded from the wealth and binding force of the literate culture. The difference with France is arresting. Statistics tell us that the 'average Frenchman', certainly outside a few urban centres, reads very few books. Though *France-Culture* has a radio schedule of a generosity and standard which no other major public broadcasting rivals, television is notoriously banal and circumspect. Yet for a number of historical and psychological reasons, some of which are inseparable from a background of conscious Latinity, Napoleonic centralization, and a persistent current of chauvinism, the less educated Frenchman does feel that he has a stake in the linguistic-literary genius of his society. The tie may be naively visual: those innumerable statues of writers and cultural worthies, those streets named after anyone who has 'made the language live'. But the relation also operates at a much subtler level: in the curious pride taken by the population at large in matters of style and correctness, in the general ear for eloquence, in the insistence, even at lower levels of commercial and bureaucratic discourse on a certain classicism and delicacy of form. *Le bien parler* is not the possession of a single or politically-eroded caste. In British society access to 'the best that has been thought and said' has often been fiercely narrow. But unless such access is widened, the social rancours which now divide the community will not find a common ground for collaborative debate. The consequences can be drastic. A semi-literate democracy is a contradiction in terms. A political society cut off from the excellence of its own past is a barbarism. Thus a Great Britain which could not draw from its own language resources of stability and influence, reserves of shared remembrance and expectation far greater than those offered by ramshackled economic manipulations, would indeed be a Britain self-betrayed.

The practical effects of such a conviction, especially, decisively, at the school-level, are problematic as well as costly. They look quixotic at a time when education is being made a favourite target of administrative myopia or, dare one say it, class vengeance. I have, in an address to last year's Headmasters' Conference,[1] tried to sketch a possible syllabus for a more effective literacy, assigning in it a central role to the history and usage of the English language. Well taught, this history can of itself exemplify and express, better than any other discipline, the key relations between the individual and society, between stability and innovation, between the spirit of place and the agencies of global diffusion. It is on a shared grasp and sense of these relations that our future may depend. But far more is involved than the school syllabus and the economics of primary and secondary education (absolutely crucial as these are). And here one's suggestions are almost bound to be piecemeal and amateurish. They would address themselves to a more inspired, more consciously illuminating use of the mass media

---

1. 'What is an Educated Man Now?', *Conference*, Vol. 12, No. 1, February, 1975.

in regard to the dissemination and exemplification of literate ideals. They would pertain to the threatened condition of quality publishing and of the book-trade in this country, emphasizing how quickly Britain is losing its leadership in the field of low-cost book-production both at the minority level and for the great hunger of the popular market. A good bookshop is already half a university (perhaps more). Yet in many places in this land there are no serious bookshops at all, no shelves for the eye and the hand to chance upon what it did not know existed. And in so many other places, bookshops which once carried out their essential task of education and of wonder are turning into glorified tobacconists.

Seeking remedies, one's mind turns with uneasy fascination to the achievements of the Soviet Union and of those East European societies which stumbled into the twentieth century with massive burdens of sub-literacy and cultural deprivation. The pace and impact of educational efforts in these communities, the genuine centrality of the classics and of the act of reading in the Leninist and Marxist-nationalist scheme of things are not in doubt. Nowhere else are the serious theatre, the symphony orchestra, the public library and lecture-hall so vital a presence in daily life. Nowhere else is the writer, the poet even, published on so vast a scale and listened to with such urgent attention. But at what political price?

As this nation transforms its economic-social fabric, education in the widest sense—signifying the realization of the self through conscious participation in a linguistic-cultural inheritance too long accessible only to the few—may become Britain's principal industry and export. (Already there is a true sense in which the model and practice of the BBC or of the Open University are a more valuble export than any shown in the trade figures.) The need to re-think the organic functions of English in the educational process, in the recomposition of a viable unity, or coherent plurality of social attitudes, is a pressing, utterly absorbing task. Both the promise and the warning are eloquent in a sentence from Wordsworth's *Essay on Epitaphs*:

> Language, if it do not uphold, and feed, and leave in quiet, like the power of gravitation or the air we breathe, is a counterspirit, unremittingly and noiselessly at work, to subvert, to lay waste, to vitiate, and to dissolve.

Or, more simply, to be, just now, a teacher of English in Britain is, indeed, a calling. Would that our political masters had a clearer notion of what is at stake.[2]

Further Reading

Richard Hoggart, *The Uses of Literacy*, 1957.
F. R. Leavis, *The Common Pursuit*, 1952.
Q. D. Leavis, *Fiction and the Reading Public*, 1932.
George Steiner, *Language and Silence*, 1967.
George Steiner, *After Babel*, 1975.
Raymond Williams, *The Long Revolution*, 1961.

2. This paper first appeared on 6 September 1975 as the printed version of a Presidential Address to the English Association.

Literature in Society

RAYMOND WILLIAMS

I want to begin by emphasizing that this title is a deliberate choice in preference to the more usual formulation of literature *and* society. The reasons for this can, I think, be briefly explained. We have only to look at the formulation literature *and* society to notice that it presupposes that society exists as a formed whole before the literature exists, that society is something which is essentially complete before its literature comes to be written. This position can only be sustained if we use an extremely narrow and damaging definition of society.

There is a comparable case in the formulation of the individual and society which I have repeatedly criticized. It is true that we can recognize certain experiences, certain levels of activity, as more or less individual on the one hand, more or less social on the other; but it is necessary also to recognize that individual and social experiences and activities are always closely interrelated. It is better to see a kind of spectrum in which we may discern at the one end a more individual activity, and at the other end a more social activity, but with no sharp or definite dividing line between the two, and always with the realization that individual and social experiences are intrinsically interconnected.

Now if this is the case, we can say that so important an activity and experience as literature is equally both individual *and* social. And so I speak of literature *in* society rather than literature *and* society, because this last formulation has one immediate detrimental effect. You will find that in most examinations of the relation of literature to society, the above impairing assumptions are put into the practice of reading and analysis whereby it is supposed that the society exists before the literature is written, that you can discover certain facts of a fixed kind about a society, and then to those facts you relate the literature; that is to say, what has then to be seen as the *subsequent* literature. This organization ignores the reality which is that in any given phase of common experience writers are sharing the life of their society. Society is not something fixed beyond them but their activity is an activity *within* it.

I find extremely unsatisfactory those modes of reading and analysis which presuppose that the forms of society are fixed before the literature comes to be written. The most common presupposition of this kind is found in orthodox Marxism in which the features of a given society are described, its particular social relations, its class character and so on delineated, and then the literature which was written during that period is related to these with more or less sophistication. I find that unacceptable for the reasons given—namely, that the making of the literature is part of the social process itself. The society cannot be said to exist until the literature, like all other activities which are part of what we understand by society, has been written.

But it is not only in orthodox Marxism that we find this misunderstanding. It is equally evident in the familiar formulation which has been common in English critical work, especially in that of the Cambridge English School, where literature is related to what is called its 'background'. Here again in practice, although this need not have been so, 'the background' is supposed to be a general body of facts against which this foreground of activity we call literature is undertaken. The background is regarded—with all the implications of the metaphor—as a fixed unchanging scene, and against this the more significant activities of the making of literature are engaged in. So that, in denying the active relationship and interrelationship between literature and other social experiences and practices, we are cut off from considering what in fact are the real relations, the primary relations, between literary practice and other kinds of individual and social experiences and practices.

Of course we can say that literature is one particular practice and that we are asking what the relations of this practice are to the rest of social activity. Now I want to meet this question quite directly, but I can only do so by pointing out that the term literature has a specific and interesting history which we have to understand if we are not to be trapped into extremely limiting definitions.

The term literature seems to emerge in the Renaissance essentially in relation to the printed book. Literature in that sense is a specialized version of what had previously been the larger field of rhetoric or discourse, which had included the arts of speaking and writing. It is not only the coming of printing and the distribution of the printed book which produced this secondary concept of literature; it is also certain attitudes towards the making of literature itself as it came to be defined. Nevertheless, we have to observe that a particular kind of discourse in writing ordinarily associated with distribution in print was separated out in the Renaissance as literature. And then we find that in the second half of the eighteenth century, and particularly during the nineteenth century, this already narrowed definition was further narrowed. That is to say, in the earlier eighteenth century, philosophy, for example, was regarded as a branch of literary production and it was commonly referred to as such. Further, the essay and certain kinds of general discourse were ordinarily regarded as contributions to literature.

A specialized meaning that represented another stage in its restriction, never quite absolute but in practice quite firm, was that of literature as *imaginative* literature, as it sometimes came to be called. That is to say, for greater precision during the period of transition, literature was not the whole practice of writing related to printed distribution; rather, literature was that kind of writing which was more specialized as imaginative—the novel, the poem, the play. It was always recognized that there were also certain marginal areas like the essay, like certain kinds of biography, or autobiography, and so on, which were also literature. Nevertheless, with increasing emphasis, a literary quality was understood as an imaginative quality. Thus you have several stages of narrowing: first, from the whole body of discourse in speech and writing, to literature as writing distributed by print; secondly, to literature as part of that writing which is recognized as imaginative. Then, thirdly, towards the end of the nineteenth century, and with greater force during our own century, there was yet a further specialization in which literature was taken to be imaginative writing distributed by print, but only that part of such writing which had certain values, a certain level of seriousness, that is to say, which in general terms was approved as of a level to be called literature. As a consequence you get statements of a kind which would have been incomprehensible earlier, such as that this work *becomes* literature or *is* literature; that this is achievement *as* literature, it has literary qualities. These phrases are understood as indicating a certain achieved level of what could now be particularized as the literary imagination.

This is where we now are, or appear to be, although I am tempted to add a fourth specialization which has sometimes been evident to me in the last twenty-five years: literature is understood as not only that writing which is distributed by print, not only imaginative writing within that category, and not only imaginative writing within that category which is felt to have achieved a certain level of seriousness and value, but also a form of writing which is no longer possible. People have spoken so much of the decline of literature, of the disappearance of literary value, of the swamping of literature by what are called modern means of communication or mass communication, that one sometimes gets the impression that the full specialist definition of literature is that it is something which was written in the past. So literature would be writing distributed in print of an imaginative kind, reaching a certain level of value and seriousness, and written in the past. Certainly, reading from contemporary critics of significance, one has the impression that literature has come to resemble that proverbial bird which flies in ever-decreasing circles until it finally and fundamentally disappears.

Now I believe that for a considerable time it has been impossible to sustain any of the specialized definitions except from a very pared down point of view which is concerned to retain certain past values, often literary values, as a kind of substitute for social values, with an essential indifference to what else has been happening in modern social life. In the real practice of writing and speaking there have been important changes. First, it has been true since the late nineteenth century that the restriction of literature to print is unsustainable. Always there has been the significant exception of drama, which in its great periods was writing for speaking, although it might also be printed. The revival of drama in the late nineteenth century introduced a whole new area in which a very specific form of writing which was *not* for distribution by print in the first instance had to be recognized as literature. Moreover, there were other developments which re-emphasized the oral constituents of discourse by writing—the practice of speaking poems, indeed of conceiving them orally at times (as in the current generation), and all kinds of associated developments in performance. Then there is the fact that in broadcasting in sound and on television we have a great body of writing that is orally transmitted only, or which has been written as a stage in a certain kind of visual realization. Furthermore, notable developments have occurred in an area somewhere between what is conventionally called fiction and what is conventionally called documentary. Here work of real significance has been produced which doesn't fit the inherited specialized categories. As a result people get tied up in knots with *genre* classifications of the documentary novel, or of factual fiction, and things of that kind, which would not have presented any difficulty before the narrowing of the basic definition of literature itself took place, and particularly before the primary definition of discourse by writing was lost. These developments have to be recognized and assessed in our own terms, because I think it is self-deception to assume that we can dispose of them by reiterating the formula inherited from the nineteenth century. The truth is that we cannot attend to discourse, especially indeed imaginative discourse, in our own time unless we push beyond the limited definitions of an earlier period.

Now if I were asked to suggest a definition by which the practice of discourse in writing could be recognized in social terms, I would suggest communication. I do believe that we have to see all forms of discourse, in speech and writing, as acts of social communication, but we must be careful not to adopt a simplistic model of communication. A simple model of communication would be that A communicates something to B, or to C, D, E, and so on, and our attention could be directed by that definition just to the relation between A and B, or A and the series from B. However, in fact we know from our literary experience that it is not only the relation between A and B that matters, but also the substance of the relationship, in this case the matter that is being communicated. If we reduce literary practice to the simple act of communication, the relationship between writer and reader, then we may find it very difficult to see in any full sense the work which is the substance of the communication. Yet equally we cannot abstract the work from the relationship between the writer and the reader. Essentially my position is that we have to see these as aspects of a single moment, both that of the relationship between writer and reader (or of writers and readers), and that of the substance of this communication (what we are in the habit of calling the work).

Emphasis on both aspects of communication is necessary because Anglo-American criticism in the last half century has abstracted the substance of communication to such a degree that it deals only in isolated works. This specialization began to occur in critical writing in the 1920s, when literature was always in practice envisaged as an isolated object, as a particular, individual artefact, and this was made to stand for the whole activity of discourse by writing. As we know, this tendency of reducing the practice of literature to the production of objects did allow a certain necessary attention to the work in itself as it really is, to quote the ordinary formulation. But the emphasis had extremely damaging effects as this critical position developed in the later stages of the New Criticism (and in contemporary Structuralist criticism), when the work was abstracted as a separate object, analysed as such, and its properties were seen as the components of the object. Moreover, when people then asked questions about the relation of literature to society, literature to psychology or biography, or literature to human nature, they looked in practice for the components within this object which could be recognized as pre-existing. They looked for social, political and economic features, they looked at elements in this man's life, they looked for archetypes and myths in a collective psychology, or they looked for permanent elements in a permanent human nature. In other words, the practice of writing was being treated as an object. The effect of this was firstly to reduce the *active* nature of all literary production. Secondly, it inevitably made subsidiary, incidental, almost indifferent, questions of the relations between writers and readers, and of the relations between writers' social experiences and other social experiences—questions which always arise from the experiences of reading and writing, but which under the pressure of this theory were asked in a compromised or compromising form. This was sustained, of course, by a particular definition of the act of reading in which the reader was presupposed as a consumer, indeed a consumer of objects.

The first mode of this definition was that of taste: certain objects were tasted on the palate (a trivial definition as Wordsworth pointed out long enough ago). The more elevated version of taste was sensibility. This version, however, involved essentially the same operation, in that objects impinged upon, or were directed to, the sensibility of a particular reader and were valued in those terms. And then, in some particular forms of modern criticism, the effects of this object on its consumer, the poem on the reader, were assessed by a kind of psychological measurement, psychometry, as in the work of I. A. Richards on impulses. So that in the later New Criticism and in Structuralism we find the kinds of speculation where, on the one hand, the practice of discourse in writing has been abstracted to an object, and on the other hand, the practice of reading has been abstracted to a kind of impersonal, ahistorical examination—the tasting, sensing, reception of an object. Indeed, it is extraordinary how most modern critical theory is a theory of consumption. Added to this, there is a strong presumption that most literature was written in the past anyway, that sadly it is a thing that is essentially over, and that there is nothing *but* objects to refer to.

The extraordinary neglect of the subject of production in modern academic literary thought and in conventional literary thought is attributable to this notion of literature as an object and as existing in the past. Interest in the active process of making is suppressed in favour of the more negotiable activity of responding to an object. Now I believe that the processes of production, the production of discourse in writing, are always fundamental; any writer is bound to see it in this way and he is not really going to be stopped, although he may at first be overawed, by these confident definitions emanating from universities which have so specialized and objectified literature that it is very difficult to think of literature in terms of a man sitting down with pen and paper and making something. I believe that the emphasis on practice is now crucial and that the neglect of practice is a contributory factor to our cultural crisis, rather than, as is so readily assumed, a symptom of one's defence of the highest cultural values.

There is a further point about the conception of literature as a series of objects which relates to a wider problem in aesthetic theory. In certain arts, notably the visual arts, what survives as a work *is* in one sense an object. When a particular painting, a particular sculpture, a particular building survives, it is there as a material object, even though its status has been to some degree, although not absolutely, affected by modern processes of reproduction. Nevertheless, in those fields it is possible to think of the work as an object and to project that simple material fact to a much wider notion of the work of art as object with certain aesthetic implications.

But we have at once to observe that in the case of literature we do not have objects in anything like the same sense. It is true that we have original manuscripts, we have first editions and so on. But we do not think of them as 'the work' in the way that we think of a particular painting or sculpture or building as 'the work'. Indeed, there is no *Hamlet*, no *Brothers Karamazov*, no *Wuthering Heights* in the sense that there is the Pietà, a painting of the Assumption, a statue of David, or a Parthenon. The very fact that the distribution of writing through print meant the widespread reproduction of objects which are taken to have equal status already affects this. Of course, it is true that scholars have to check these copies, as we would call them, to see that they are as accurate as may be in relation to the original manuscript, the first edition and so on. Nevertheless, we do not regard the copy of a work as some kind of inferior reproduction of it. It has, once it has been checked for accuracy, the same status as the original.

But this is only a minor point. The more important point is that in literary practice, because of the nature of poetic writing, we have in any case not an object but a notation, and this is true not only as regards alphabetic writing, but also in the much more general sense that all writing is a set of notations within certain known conventions.

This is particularly evident in the case of a piece of dramatic writing, which cannot be truly understood as a piece of writing for performance or for reading unless the conventions which are embodied in it, or often assumed in it, are grasped. Where these conventions are familiar we get a sense of easy transition; where they are unfamiliar, as in Greek tragedy or Elizabethan drama, we have to learn them. We have to become conscious of these conventions as the necessary accompaniment to the notations that seem to be the text.

The same is true of all other forms of writing, where certain conventions of sentence structure and of punctuation, certain conventions of narrative and of tense operate. Indeed, certain conventions involving expectation about the nature of the discourse are intrinsic to the practice. What we receive as a notation when the conventions are familiar, when the transition from the notation to the act of reading seems immediate and direct, we falsely describe as natural. In practice, however, as we can see most evidently when the conventions are unfamiliar (both in very old and very new work), the conventional element of the notation is crucial; it is already a radical social element within the literary practice itself which has to be understood not as a secondary but as a primary matter. And I believe that one of the key areas of the study of literature *in* society is the study of just these conventions and the practice of notation.

Now there is a further and familiar question about literature in society, which has to do with its value *in* society, its value *to* society, its status *in* society—that whole range of questions. Here it is equally necessary to propose some new ways of looking at the matter. If one reads only aesthetic theory, or what passes for aesthetic theory in modern practice, one gets a certain elevated notion of literature which corresponds to the final stage of specialized definitions alluded to earlier; literature as the production of higher consciousness, as the enactment of the highest values, as sensibility at its finest and most active, and so on. Now this is all very well, provided you stay with the definition of literature which is so reduced that it is the embodiment of the highest values or the representation of the highest consciousness, and that this is presumed by your initial definition. You have defined it as that, and you find it is indeed that, and you can go happily around that circle in aesthetic theory with this stress on literature as the highest consciousness, or quite often, as the newest consciousness, and within its limited terms, this always works.

However, there is then a considerable problem in attending to the whole range of literature. It is my constant experience that one can find what seem to be satisfactory definitions, often satisfactory because they are circular in the context of the aesthetic theory referred to above, but which come to fade more and more in the mind as one goes to the actual experience of reading within the whole range of novels, poems, plays and the like. The new novel, the new play, the new poem—is it fair to it to expect it to carry the weight of these elevated definitions? In a sense, I think, some of these definitions crush the very values which they offer to point to. In any case I think that if we are to attend, as I believe we must (if we are serious in our study of literature and in our study of the practice of English too) to the whole range of writing, and indeed of speech, of discourse in writing and speech, then these limiting definitions are of little use to us.

I would like to argue at this point that we have to consider a culture in a different way if we are to be in a position to describe the full range of literary practice and to go on from that to any realistic description of meanings and values.

The way I would put it is this. I believe that in any society in a particular period there is a common body of meanings and values which include for the purposes of literary practice certain definite conventions from which certain notations can be read. These are conventions not only of meaning but also of value, and this common core of meanings and values and practices can be called the corporate culture of a period. It could be called the common culture, but I would prefer to call it the corporate culture, because it is essentially the fact that it has been taken into a common body, a common body which is lived in contemporary social practice. The meanings and values seem, while the corporate culture is being lived, natural, real, expressing the sense of what it is at that time to be human.

There is no presumption of value about a particular corporate culture. It may have a very high value; it may, in a bad period, in a bad time, have a much lower value. These are properly questions of cultural history. What I am trying to distinguish is the notion of the existence of a corporate culture. And I believe that it is true that this corporate culture never includes the whole range of meanings and values which are active in society. It never includes even all the significant practices in the society. Indeed, that is what incorporation means, namely, that it is a selection and organization of certain definite meanings and values.

How can we describe those areas which are not in this sense corporate? Well, first we have to notice residual meanings and values, that is to say, meanings and values which are essentially the result of earlier and different phases of living, phases of experience, phases of society. Such residual meanings and values are, however, still active, and often the more active where they represent particular meanings and values which the current corporate culture for some reason does not fully or adequately represent. It is very important to stress this residual element because it is my belief that much literary practice in the twentieth century, and certainly much literary study, has been in this sense highly residual. That is not a moral observation, nor is any implication involved. It is simply as a result of historical analysis that we can say that meanings and values are more regularly derived from the past than from the present system of meanings and values, that is, the one that is actually operative at the core of contemporary society.

Then there is also an area of emergent meanings and values, that is to say, of practices, extractions of significance, which again diverge from the contemporary corporate culture in a radically different way from residual practice. These attempt to create new meanings, new significance, new values, new practices in direct literary terms by creating new conventions and new notations. Often the imputation of novelty to literature is an imputation derived from the experience of this kind of emergent culture which is always important in a period but which is also always a quite small part of literary practice.

If, then, we see a corporate culture, a residual culture, and an emergent culture (all of these of course to be understood as active practices rather than static areas), we are in a position to begin a different kind of social analysis of literary practice. But I think we can only do this if we introduce another notion which is necessary, namely, that of incorporation.

Now I believe it is true that a successful corporate culture, a system of meanings and values which offers to be the core of a particular lived society, has to include at least some versions of the past which make sense at some depth. It may also have to include some versions of the future, or of what is emergent, but that is less fundamental. In relation to the past there is a constant process of incorporation, what I have called elsewhere the selective tradition. So that when *the* tradition, or the *high* tradition, is spoken of in relation to literature, what is always meant (although it is not always admitted) is a selective tradition; that is to say, from the whole experience of the past, in this case the vast range of the practice of writing, certain things are selected, and by the same token certain things are excluded or neglected. This is rationalized as selection by time, but in fact if you look at what an active and contentious process this is, involving the re-reading of the past of English literature, for example, you will see that it is always a selection according to certain active meanings and values. These are sometimes corporate, sometimes residual, but in any case the selection is a selection by men in relation to meanings and values which ought to be made explicit and indeed *have* to be made explicit in the end.

So that a tradition is always a selective tradition. That is to say, it is continually being re-made; there is a continual selection and re-selection of ancestors, and beyond the simple fact of inclusion or exclusion there is a constant process of re-reading, re-interpretation, which constitutes a large part of what is called critical activity. Here again, we see incorporation taking place in the sense that the works are being read through the meanings and values of the contemporary corporate culture.

Indeed, there is often great tension between this process and the work of scholars who in a more archaeological spirit attempt to reconstruct what they insist are the original meanings and values if they can so separate themselves from the culture of their own time as to do this. There is great tension between what they insist are the original meanings and values and what other people insist are the meanings and values that are now active, that is to say, that have become active within a system of meanings and values that is now operative. This necessary incorporation is part of a process which can be described in more critical ways where incorporation into a system of meanings and values has always to do with a particular wider organization of society, with the ratification of certain natural or necessary social relations, certain kinds of institutions and so on; and much necessary critical analysis has to do with tracing the often sinuous path between the re-interpretation as meanings and values, and the functions of these re-interpretations as social ratification or social incorporation.

One last point about the practice of literature in society. I believe, in the light of what I have been saying, that it is necessary to regard the practice of literature as both the practice of a collective mode and the practice of what are in effect innumerable individual projects. What has most exercised me is to find a mode of reading, a mode of response, which is capable of recognizing both the collective mode and the individual project, without reducing any individual project to a collective mode, or seeing literature as an endless series of individual projects without recognition of anything but the more *abstract* collective modes.

These collective modes are in the first instance the conventions of which I have already spoken. They sometimes materialize as *genre* but they are not only *genre* because very often within a period there is a community across which *genre* is equally collective. There are the conventions, the common practices, the common expectations, the common strategies of literature in a period, and there is the reality of the individual projects which in this important sense could not be undertaken without them, although the making of new collective modes from a minority of individual projects is part of the real history of literature. At the same time the individual projects are never wholly reducible to collective modes, because it is only in their practice, their irreducible practice, that the collective modes are active.

Now it is for the purpose of recognizing the reality of both of these moments of the literary practice, that I began to use the term 'structure of feeling', and my concluding remarks must be about this.

I do not believe that one can relate literary practice simply to a pre-existing society, as I explained at the beginning, or to component properties of a society, or to its leading ideas and so on. Most literature operates in the area of common meanings and values which is the corporate culture. Some of it is residual, some (a small part) emergent, but the reality of any corporate culture which is going to persist is that it is continually changing. New experiences, new relations, new responses, new practices mean that it is in a continuous process of change. And in relation to this I think we have to recognize a category that I would call the pre-emergent, where the recognition of new experiences, new possible practices, new relations and possible relations, is apprehended but not yet articulated. Indeed, the emergent literature of a period is the articulation in what often seem very isolated and lonely ways at first, of something which is nevertheless coming into social existence, that which I call pre-emergent. This structure of feeling is so called because it is essentially different from the structure of what is already known and formed and articulated. It is often apprehended as an isolated and individual, a private feeling; it is often what is felt by members of society but not confessed, because in a sense there are no forms for it yet, or because of difficulties of recognition or acceptance. The sense that one often has in some of the very newest literature is that it is articulating something which one has already felt but felt without this articulation.

This area of inter-relations—the problem of discerning the pre-emergence of a structure of feeling, which, once it has passed into history, is recognizable as a collective mode, and is seen as a real structure which unites individuals who may not have been aware of each other, which unites works composed without relation to each other—needs, of course, much further and more detailed examination. But in the end if we are asking about the significant relations of literature *in* society, we have to attend in an active way to the whole range that I have been describing.

Yet perhaps the most interesting part of this enquiry will be into this pre-emergent phase in which new structures of feelings are creating new practices of writing.

Further Reading

W. Benjamin, *Illuminations*, 1963.
L. Goldmann, *Towards a Sociology of the Novel*, 1974.
S. C. Heath, *The Nouveau Roman*, 1972.
G. Lukács, *The Historical Novel*, 1960.
Raymond Williams, *The Country and the City*, 1973.

The Poetics of Biography

LEON EDEL

They were standing on the steps of the British Museum, a little to one side away from the usual loungers. It was a day when the sunshine in Bloomsbury was less watery than usual; the warmth was irresistible. What they really resisted was returning to the great circular cavern where so many persons were taking information out of books simply to put it into books. There was Criticus, a short, thick-bodied intellectual with spectacles, who clung to a pipe in his right hand. There was Poeticus, who cultivated a Yeatsian forelock, but without the eyeglasses and the ribbon. He made his living by reviewing and had come to the B.M. to look up something or other. Then there was Plutarchus, a lean and lanky biographer wearing a corduroy jacket. His bushy brows made him seem like some furry animal who liked to burrow—in manuscripts. They talked of this and that, smoking many cigarettes in moments of long silence. Poeticus wrinkled his eyes in the sun and buried his seamed, turtle-like face in his turtleneck sweater, pushing his chin down hard, and he wondered how Plutarchus could burrow so long in the life of the dead in order to write of life. He mentioned casually that George Eliot thought biographers to be a disease of English literature, and Plutarchus, on the defensive, retorted that writing a life was like writing a poem except that one used prose, and followed the modes of the novelist. Poets, he said, were too secretive; they buried their lives in their poems, and made eternal mysteries of the mind. Writers of lives ferret out their mysteries and this doubtless made them objectionable. He added he didn't see why biography couldn't be regarded as a job of work, quite as respectable and difficult as any other job, rarely well done, most of the time leaving a great deal to be desired.

With this the three, idling on the steps and reluctant to return to the cavern, lapsed into an ever-deepening exchange on the necessities for criticism, the nature of poesy, the *raison d'être* of biography. Criticus was voluble; he said that Plutarchus

would have to admit that not all lives are interesting and that
therefore many are not worth writing. Plutarchus granted this.
A biographer chose his subject, unless he were a hack, because
he was drawn to it, 'you as a critic, unless you are doing hack
work, are also drawn to this writer rather than that; you don't
just pick writers and subjects indiscriminately, like some Ph.D.
candidate.' And he went on, again a bit defensively, to say Criticus ought to allow biography the same privileges he allowed
himself. Poeticus was silent. His eyes wandered to a taxi which
released an auburn-haired young woman, obviously American,
who wore ear-rings and carried an armful of folders and an
attaché case. She glanced at the rum-looking trio as her long
legs flashed past them and disappeared, presumably into the
cavern. Poeticus mused. Why did so much femininity require
brainwork and in the B.M.? Criticus shrugged his shoulders.
Plutarchus, however, suggested they ought not change the subject. 'What I've been thinking,' he said, 'is that there are moun-
tains of books on critical theory, and we've had all manner of
poetics since Aristotle—take Dryden's *Of Dramatic Poesy*—but no
one has ever written what could truly be called a poetics of biography.' The pedants sometimes wrote little books on how they
had done their research; they sometimes even called research
an 'art', but as for poetics, the true making and the true finding,
all the exquisite fabric wrought out of inanimate materials, no
one seemed to want to talk about this. It was all taken for
granted.

Poeticus: Do you know why?

Plutarchus: Yes, I know why. Because you do not want the
poet in his poem, although he stares at you within and between
the lines. You try to pretend that poetry is impersonal; you give
poetry readings before audiences and on television so that your
face is better known than your lines, and you talk about how
you wrote each poem, and then you pretend the poem is impersonal. You blandly offer us autobiography, and yet relegate biography, one of the most beautiful of the arts because it seeks
the truth so directly, to the infirmary, where George Eliot put
it. You give it so low a place that usually only journeymen prac-
tise it, as Lytton Strachey said, and they produce indigestible
volumes which you can then condemn as indigestible. You
don't seem to care that a biography shall have a shape or a
form, a direction, and an overall economy—all the things that

you, Criticus, talk about constantly and all the things you, Poeticus, do in your poems, for it is second nature to you. But I've never heard you ask for them in a biography.

Poeticus: I'll tell you why: biographies of writers, whether written by others, *or* by themselves, are always superfluous and usually in bad taste.

Plutarchus: Spare us your plagiarism. This is not you speaking; it's W. H. Auden.

Poeticus: Yes; but I agree with him; and when I agree I appropriate. It's in Auden's commonplace book, *A Certain World*, in the preface, the very first sentence.

Plutarchus: The title of the book gives him away, and his preface, which I've read, seems almost capriciously to confuse readers. Whose 'certain world'? Auden's, of course. The book is autobiography, or at least filled with large quantities of it.

Poeticus: But probably in *good* taste.

Plutarchus: Let's omit questions of taste. We know there's bad taste and good taste, and sometimes very little. Even some of your poems, when you resort to four letter words, as if our language were poverty-stricken, show what a brave infant you can be; but infants are not renowned for having good taste or bad taste.

Criticus: Stick to the point. I agree with Poeticus. Biography is neither relevant to literary study nor to criticism. The critic doesn't need biography to perform the critical act. What was it the reviewer called biography the other day in the *T.L.S.*, the issue that had my picture on the front page? Yes, he said biography was 'gossip made permanent'. I thought that rather witty.

Plutarchus: Doubtless; and we could say that some forms of criticism are spleen made permanent. Permanency is a relative matter. You want me to stick to the question? I will. A biography contains some gossip; sometimes it has a voyeuristic quality; and sometimes it is badly written, and sometimes it is well written. But isn't this true of all writings? We take the good with the bad and there's always too much of the bad. Good taste resides in the final judgements we must pass, the standards and rules we discover for our πoιητικη. But why does Wystan say that literary biographies and autobiographies, that is, lives of writers, are superfluous? Perhaps he shares my belief. The poet gives himself away in his poem, and therefore a biographi-

cal commentary or interlinear *is* superfluous. But we can turn
this around: if a poem is a piece of autobiography, and if I
choose to see the poet in his poem, that's my privilege once he
prints the poem or reads it to me. Must I close my eyes to
the images you offer me? I like to quote Thoreau, a curious
American provincial. In an inspired moment he said that
poetry is 'a piece of very private history, which unostentatiously
lets us into the secret of a man's life.' Or that other provincial,
Edgar Allen Poe, who argued that it's wrong to suppose that
the book of an author is a thing apart from the author. How
odd of Auden....

Criticus: Well, you know Auden wasn't being rigid about it.
He sometimes reviewed biographies; in his last review he said,
'As a rule I am opposed to biographies of writers, but in
Trollope's case, for a number of reasons, I approve.'

Plutarchus: Apparently, then, biographers must obtain their
seal of approval from Mr Auden and from other poets. Let's
get back to the question of the poetics.

Poeticus: A boring subject.

Plutarchus: Poets are bored by biographers, but they read
them under the table. And, Criticus, has it ever occurred to
you that literary critics are notoriously poor biographers?

Criticus: I could give you a list of modern critics as long as
your arm, and longer, who've written good biographies.

Plutarchus: Spare me your lists. Besides all the biographies
on your list are defective. Critics seem to think a biography must
include everything. They have no perspective, no logic, no
method. And do you know why critics are bad biographers?
I'll tell you. Because criticism is a more egotistical, power-
seeking trade than biography. The critic asserts himself by explaining and discussing the work of others. Few critics are
disinterested. The critic is rather (as Marcellus of France
called him) an incomplete man who completes himself with
the work of another. The work has to exist before a critic can
begin to function.

Criticus: Proust was insulting. I could say biographers are incomplete men who complete themselves by writing the lives of
others.

Plutarchus: Not quite. Cocteau once said the artist is a kind
of prison from which the works of art escape. The biographer
is the historian of that imprisonment, and also of that liberation.

And then biographers can't afford the luxury of egotism. They must possess a capacity for sympathy and empathy; it's their precious stock-in-trade. This sometimes makes them poor critics. Criticism, by its very nature, can't afford to be too empathic, not if it is to be judicial and evaluative. Your ideal biographer writes a story of the progress of a life; he must allow himself to feel its failures, its obstacles overcome, its human ambiguities, its fallibilities, and the drama of personality and temperament. If he's a good biographer he knows how to select and use significant detail. He can't allow himself to be too much the critic, lest his critiques of the work impede the march of the story. A critical biography is a contradiction in terms. To tell a good story, to summarize documents with vividness and sharpness, and not to quote wholesale from them (as the helpless do, neither having a sense of form nor being skilled in the art of writing), and to do it in lively prose, this requires more than most biographers know or can do. To this extent Auden is right. Bad work is always in bad taste. The beauty of what a biographer does resides in his insights: we discern the complexities of being, without pretending that life's riddles have been answered.

Poeticus: You are right, Plutarchus. I find it wholly understandable that critics are often poor biographers; but then they are poor poets and poor novelists as well. Yet poets and novelists are often good critics, and could be good biographers, because they speak with authority from their workshop. It's the status of biographers that Auden throws into question, the very job. Critics often think they are on Olympus, and biographers think they are God since they try to refashion human stuff, but you must face the fact that we all have our vanities, and critical and poetical vanity relegates biography to second-class citizenship. Why else do you have to defend yourself so vehemently in this noonday warmth? Write your poetics. It won't help. You won't reform anyone. You'll still be condescended to, even by me, because we all think we know the truths about someone else's life, and don't need biographers to tell us.

Criticus: Why do you treat critics with such contempt? In what way, Plutarchus, have they injured you?

Plutarchus: They haven't injured me: it is their logic I find hard to swallow. I know one critic who argued that the life of Joyce—or was it James—was too long, and that the biographer had not shown a sense of proportion. After all, the critic said, Tolstoy and Flaubert were more important than Joyce or James and *they* didn't have such long biographies. That's an example of what critics do—the stockmarket school of criticism. Must I tailor my biography to their current devaluations? One year the Snowman's stock is high, and the next year the Greene man's; biographers would indeed be in a quandary if they followed such bullish and bearish trends. A biography takes its length not only from an artist's importance, but from the documents available. If you took Tolstoy as a measure, what length would you give Corvo? He would have to be a footnote, and yet one of the most interesting biographies of modern times has been *The Quest for Corvo*.

Criticus: Please, let's not fight old battles. I propose that we proceed in a systematic and objective way. Plutarchus, show us your stuff. Take this book. Demonstrate what you would do with it. It's the best way to give us a poetics of biography.

Plutarchus took the book which Criticus hauled out from his briefcase. He read the title, *A Certain World, A Commonplace Book*, by W. H. Auden.

Criticus: There you are. Give us a brief biography.

Plutarchus: Willingly. It's easier than you think. Unlike critics who decide they can become biographers overnight, I've had a long apprenticeship. And I know my way around this book. My own copy—I wish I had it with me—is pencil-scarred. But Wystan has supplied good headings, alphabetically arranged, so I can find what I want. I'll show you what I mean when I say this is autobiography. Auden tentatively admits as much in his foreword, where he says a writer's private life 'is, or should be, of no concern, to anybody except himself, his family and his friends.' Of no concern except to himself. But how can he then remain silent, since the total concern of a poet is *himself* talking to the world? 'I am Goya' says Voznesensky, but he is Voznesensky too. The moment a poet starts putting on his masks he puts his heart on his sleeve, he invades his own privacy, he parades it before everyone. Auden fills this book with passages from his reading: he devotes sections to choirboys, names, prayers, dreams, nature, logic, man, and a hundred other life-subjects. 'Here is a map of my planet,' he says in his foreword, in contradiction to his statement that autobiography is superfluous. And to aid us in our study of this map he offers passages devoted to his own reflections, which he has tried, he says, to keep to a minimum. Yet he has felt some compelling need to include them. They are easily identified, for they are indented and unsigned. Everything else is sourced.

Poeticus: You propose to reconstruct Wystan Auden?

Plutarchus: Of course not. I propose simply to show you the extraordinary glimpses Auden gives us into his private world immediately after telling us that this world is not our concern. For example he tells us, in a passage I can only describe as auto-biographical, that he was both the youngest child and the youngest grandchild in his family. He was always youngest in class. This made him feel for years younger than others—the youngest perhaps—in any group. He goes on to tell us that he has now come to see, as he walks in the street, that there are younger persons in the world, and this has led him to the thought that he is aging, and that he will some day die. Let me tell you that this information has considerable significance for a biographer. Auden has given us a prime fact about himself: not that he was the youngest, but that he seems, as a consequence of being the youngest, to have moved always outside his peer group. Like James Joyce, who was the Clongowes precocity, a mere babe among older boys, Auden grew up deprived of certain elements of his childhood. The talk he heard around him seems to have been the talk of older folk; older ideas were available to him, some perhaps beyond his reach; and this suggests a kind of forcing of experience, the establishment of premature standards in his development, and premature attitudes. See at once into what complexities of being Wystan leads us. And now that he realizes he cannot be young among the old, since he is old himself he loses his sense of eternal youth— though he may live to be a hundred.[1]

And then he tells us that as a boy he enjoyed band concerts, and is filled with nostalgia when he hears a band. He possessed a voice both before and after it broke, so he sang in choirs. As a choirboy he learned not only to sight-read music but to enunciate clearly; this made him conscious of metre both in speech and song, an excellent apprenticeship. Long before he took a conscious interest in poetry, he had cultivated his ear. We learn

---

1. This paper was delivered Saturday, 1 September 1973. Auden died of a heart attack in Vienna on 28 September 1973.

also, out of his boyhood, that at boarding school he was forced
to take cold baths, a rule based on the erroneous belief that
cold water subdues carnal passion. He resolved never to take
cold baths again once he left school.

.... And so turning the pages, with long pauses as he read,
Plutarchus began a commentary on Auden's commonplace
book. He made it clear that he wasn't trying to do a vocal biography and, that anything he ended up with would not be a
life story. It was his point that the book contained certain
revelations, that it could be called 'a private world' as well as
'a certain world' but a world made no longer private. Thus
(said Plutarchus) the poet muses that if he had gone into the
church he might now be a bishop; he believes he would be
liberal in politics, but conservative in religion. He tells the story
of his patron saint, Wystan, a sort of Hamlet (or Oedipus)
figure, who objected to the uncanonical marriage of his
widowed mother to his godfather. This led to a sad ending. The
mother and her spouse got rid of Wystan, who was later sancti-
fied. And in this we have a hint of castration, struck early, to
which we will return.

Criticus: Castration? You mean infanticide.

Plutarchus: Saint Wystan's mother had him done in, because he
objected to her husband. Violent death is a supreme castration.

Poeticus: Go on, go on with your story. I find it interesting,
even if your ideas are far-fetched.

Plutarchus: It *is* interesting because it contains character, personality, temperament. We know from his poetry that Wystan
has a witty mind; he is aphoristic; his ironies are of the mind.
The passages from poets, from his general reading, from his
interest in humanism all testify to this.

Criticus: All this is obvious. Auden is simply reminiscing. Old
Possum, for all his talk of objective correlatives and the impersonality of poetry, fell into reminiscence every time he gave a
lecture. They can't help it. What of the more distinctively personal do you find in this volume?

Plutarchus: I hesitate to tread on delicate ground, but it's clear
that in the poet's 'certain world' he's most uncertain about
women. Not his feelings about them. He's quite clear about how
he feels.

Poeticus: Women *are* uncertain.

Plutarchus: I mean they appear in this book as threatening and menacing figures, like the mother of Saint Wystan. He's afraid of them.

Criticus: Facts, please.

Plutarchus: Well, when we arrive at the C category we find nothing less than an alliterative 'Castration Complex'. Don't accuse me of being Freudian. It's Auden who wrote these words in this book. He begins, 'As a child, one of my favourite books was an English translation of Dr Hoffmann's *Struwwelpeter* and my favourite poem in the book was "The Story of Little Suck-a-Thumb".' This, Criticus, is very Germanic of Auden. I couldn't help shuddering slightly that little boy Wystan should find such verses appealing, though doubtless many children do. Let me quote two of them. Mamma announces at the beginning to her little son Conrad that she must go out and leave him. Having generated a separation anxiety, she admonishes him, 'Don't suck your thumb while I'm away.'
Shall I read on? It's as German as you please:

> The great tall tailor always comes
> To little boys that suck their thumbs;
> And 'ere they dream what he's about,
> He takes his great sharp scissors out
> And cuts their thumbs clean off—and then,
> You know, they never grow again.

Small wonder, let me add, that, as soon as Mother's back is turned, Conrad's anxious little thumb pops right into Conrad's anxious little mouth. I will read you the next verse:

> The door flew open, in he ran,
> The great, long, red-legged scissor-man.
> Oh! children, see! the tailor's come
> And caught out little Suck-a-Thumb.
> Snip! Snap! Snip! They go so fast
> That both his thumbs are off at last.

Criticus: My generation read *Struwwelpeter*. Children don't experience violence as sensitively as adults: they take it in their little stride sometimes as comedy.

Plutarchus: Dear boy, I am discussing a poet's psychology, not child psychology. What's important is that in the final couplet the voice of Conrad's mother is heard on a note of triumph (there's no shock at missing thumbs):

.... I knew he'd come
To naughty little Suck-a-Thumb.

Auden quite rightly tells us, what all the psychologists have
remarked, 'Of course, it's not about thumb-sucking at all, but
about masturbation, which is punished by castration.' Yes, and
we could find further interpretations of such a nature for other
verses in Dr Hoffman's volume of adult sado-masochism
designed for children. The significance for biography resides
in Auden's choice. Out of millions of poems, out of the handful
in this popular book, the poet has singled out one and pro-
claimed it the favourite verses of his childhood. He might have
chosen the one about Cruel Frederick who kills birds and whips
his dog till the enraged animal bites him; or about Harriet who
burns herself to a small pile of ashes playing with matches in
spite of parental warnings, so that even the tears of her cats
can't extinguish the flames; or the very contemporary tale of
the beastly little boys who are dipped in ink by a socially
minded anti-racist giant, and are made very black indeed,
because they mocked and tormented a blackamoor and said,
'Oh Blacky, you're as black as ink.' There is the one about the
man who's shot at by the rabbit he tries to shoot, but the bullet
destroys the coffee cup in his wife's hand; and Fidgety Philip
who pulls the tablecloth and all the dishes over himself. All are
cautionary and coercive verse designed to frighten children into
good behaviour. One could find castration in all of them I
believe, and learned papers have been written on the subject.
Nevertheless it's little Conrad Suck-a-Thumb who is singled out
by Wystan and he then asks the proper, the scientific, the biographical question: 'Why did I enjoy the poem as a child? Why
was I not frightened?' His reason: well, he says, he simply
wasn't a thumb-sucker, but a nail-biter! If we ponder this, we
can see a characteristic masking of reality, a manoeuvre to
explain away genuine fright. There *was* fear, a great deal. The
real fear, the real ogre in the poem, isn't the red-legged scissors-
man. Auden tells us, 'I knew well that Suck-a-Thumb's fate
would not be mine, because the scissors-man was a figure in
a poem.' There is, however, a *real* person in the poem. This is
the threatening mother. And about her, Auden says nothing.
He adds, however, at the end of his analysis, 'very different is
the fear aroused in me by spiders, crabs and octopi which are,

I suspect, symbols to me for the castrating *vagina dentata*,' the tooth-filled entrapping shark-vagina. So much for the threatening fearful mother.

Poeticus: How unpleasant! How unpleasant this comparison of the fear figure to a spider, a crab, an octopus.

Plutarchus: And in a way a kind of shark.

Poeticus: But you are only speculating that the mother in the poem was the crab, or a threatening vagina.

Plutarchus: Yes, so I speculated, as biographers do, until I came to the D's. There we reach 'Dreams'. And the poet should have known better than to recite to us an old dream, a nightmare. I'm certain he's aware that nothing reveals a man's inner world and his private life more than his dreams. The symbolism of a dream is always suggestive even if we do not have the means of interpreting it. Auden tells us of his horrible nightmare with the same *sang-froid* that little Wystan showed towards the scissors-man. Remember, I'm not interpreting the dream because (a) I am not a psychoanalyst and (b) dreams cannot be interpreted *de chic*. The dreamer must supply the context. And yet this book gives us glimpses into contexts. (Plutarchus flipped the pages of the commonplace book and then read silently, to himself.) Yes, here it is. It's dated August 1936. Auden would then have been twenty-nine. He dreams he's in a hospital for an appendectomy. A removal of an appendix, any appendage indeed, is a kind of scissors-man act. The surgeon probably doesn't say 'Snip! Snap! Snip!', but the scissors are indeed converted in the dream to a surgical instrument. In the dream there was also someone with green eyes and a terrifying affection for Auden. So instead of removing the appendix, the medical scissors-man cuts off 'the arm of an old lady who was going to do me an injury.' Auden explains this to the doctors, but they aren't interested. The dream then relates an escape from the hospital and a terrified pursuit. But what's important is that two castrations have been mentioned: the threat of a removal of an appendix and the amputation of a woman's arm. A later sentence supplies a context. The dreamer has 'a vision of pursuit like a book illustration and I think,' says Auden, 'related to the long, red-legged scissors-man in *Struwwelpeter*.'

Poeticus: You are indeed invading a private life.

Plutarchus: Am I? I don't think so. All I've done is to read you a German poem captioned by Auden 'Castration Complex', and then I quoted a passage about the *vagina dentata*, and now I give you excerpts from a dream, a nightmare, recounted by the poet himself. He supplies this curious data from *his* world, and we may speculate as we wish. I'd speculate that the nightmare, filled with amputations and terror of flight and pursuit by a red-legged scissors-man (the red might even be a hint of blood, and the legs are two further appendages), suggests that the German poem *did* frighten the child terribly: Auden furnishes a great deal of penis symbolism and expresses a great and horrible fear of penis-loss. But it isn't sex that's important in this material. It's the relation of the boy to the threatening mother, the woman who first leaves the little boy alone, exposed to a danger she foretells, and almost prescribes, and the little boy who is so promptly punished. I discern in this a possible 'double-bind', not unlike Raskolnikov's, though on a different level. A fear not only of the *vagina dentata*, that is, the shark-woman, but also of his own anger and aggression against the woman with whom he has identified himself, and whom he counter-attacks by dreaming that *her* arm is cut off instead of *his* appendix. I guess I *am* doing what I said I wouldn't do, trying to interpret a dream *de chic*. So I'll pursue my researches in the book.

Criticus: You *are* being very Freu lian.

Plutarchus: Come now, Criticus. ⌐ n I? Would you consider it legitimate of me, after all this, to look at the P's simply to see what Auden may tell us about the penis? He's already mentioned the vagina.

Criticus: Why not?

Plutarchus: This is what we call 'research' in biography. One thing leads to another. (He turns the pages.) Paradise, The Earthly—hmm, here it is, right where it's supposed to be. The second item under the P's. 'Penis Rivalry.' A full page. (Plutarchus paused and read silently. Poeticus moved a little impatiently. Criticus tried to look over his shoulder.)

Criticus: Come, read it aloud.

Plutarchus: Pardon me. Well, the poet begins by wondering whether women suffer from 'penis envy'. This is, of course, pure Freud. Auden isn't sure he agrees. He then says he's quite certain that 'all males, without exception, whatever their age, suffer from *penis rivalry*', and he says that this has now become a threat to the future existence of the human race. He goes on, 'behind every quarrel between men, whether individually or collectively, one can hear the taunt of a little urchin: My prick (or my father's) is bigger than yours (or your father's) and can pee further.'

Poeticus: (Impatiently.) Must you read us this Freudian nonsense?

Criticus: Go on, go on.

Plutarchus: Well, I'll paraphrase. The poet goes on to say that nearly all weapons, from the spear and the sword to the revolver and the rocket, are phallic symbols. And then, let me quote, 'Men to be sure, also fashion traps, most forms of which are vaginal symbols, but they never take a pride in them as they do in their weapon, and, when heroes exchange gifts of friendship, weapons figure predominantly. But where, in literature, can one find a loving description of a trap, or hear of one as a precious gift?'

Criticus: I wonder whether Auden has read D. H. Lawrence.

Plutarchus: The *vagina dentata* is a form of trap. It is a barbed trap. The rest of the passage is devoted to the dangers of our phallic toys. Auden remarks, by the way, that he would prefer to leave international relations to women, preferably married ones—they being I suppose less dangerous than unmarried. Their trap is theoretically held in control by their husbands; this makes such women 'safer'.

Poeticus: Well, my dear Plutarchus, what can you do with this? Where does it lead you, and us?

Plutarchus: It can lead us very far but it's not my intention to pursue the implications of Wystan Auden's iconography in this book; his poems offer greater riches. I wonder, however— and I think it very natural of me to do so—that a poet who understands iconography so profoundly should turn the human genitals into such fixed symbols—the male a weapon and the female a trap. We know that they can take quite different forms and evoke other feelings in our imagination, the male being an object of love and fertility, of warmth-giving and seed-giving, and the female equally representing warmth and nurture and also receptivity and love. Having been given these icons, out of a poet's private world, I would, as a biographer, have to ponder their rigidity and look into his poetry for clarifications. When the poet asks *where* in literature one can find a loving description of a trap, the answer is perhaps nowhere; but when he makes that trap woman (for one cannot dissociate the vagina, as if it were a carburettor, from its possessor) then the answer is in a thousand books, in *Lady Chatterley*, even in *Hecate County*, in all the books which have celebrated forms of love, almost everywhere in Shakespeare. Think of Hamlet's fond thought of what lies between Ophelia's legs, and yet he, more than most men, feels himself trapped. And those of us, of an older generation, who once read the jejune naughtiness of *Jurgen*, can recall that Jurgen's long sword asked insistently for a sheath, not a trap. The experiences of love are infinite and complex. It's only when there's some deep trouble in the relationship that women may become traps to men, and men may become aggressors to women *and* each other. There are many kinds of male and female aggression. We call it platitudinously the war of the sexes.

Poeticus: Plutarchus, you're sadly wanting in humour. How deadly serious biographers can be! For Auden his commonplace book was a lark and you won't let him have his fun. Perhaps he scattered these symbols to prove how egregious and superfluous biographies of literary men can be?

Plutarchus: I appreciate Auden's wit. I also know that the wit and humour of the unconscious lay traps for us all. And the choices, remember, were Auden's. Some men never think of the *vagina* as *dentata*: their minds run to it as the Great Good Place. They see delicacies and softnesses in it, and who knows what else. Each man makes his own icons. And Auden, denouncing biographies of writers, constantly reviews volumes of letters, and in these reviews he shows himself an expert biographer. He sees within the letters the person, the character, in the very act of writing them. Read his essay on the Oscar Wilde letters, and you'll recognize a fine biographer buried within the poet; or at least a master of the biographical essay.

Poeticus: I still hold with Auden that all this reaching for the man behind the letters, the poet behind the poem, is really vulgar. It isn't anyone's business.

Plutarchus: Do you want me to pretend that there's no poet in the poem? Criticus is entitled to say 'This poem is bad; this poem is good.' But I'm not allowed to talk of the three or six or twenty voices in poetry which happen to be a series of *personae*? Well, I at least have Yeats to support me: he said, 'There is always a living face behind the mask.'

Criticus: Your idea of biography doesn't correspond to biography as we've always thought of it. Starting with Boswell, modern biographies offer us the routine of people's lives: what they ate for breakfast, how they played golf, how many mistresses they had, and so on. They invade privacy in every paragraph.

Plutarchus: What privacies, please, in the age of the camera? The close-up on television shows me the pimple on Poeticus's neck every time he gives a poetry reading. In my poetics I do insist that we discriminate, that we do not relate the boredom of lives, unless that boredom is part of the story (like the last half of Max Beerbohm's life), and that we recognize that biographies of exceptional persons are written because they're exceptional. Thumb-sucking is a common and natural practice among children; but when a future poet, in his childhood, admires verses about cutting off thumbs, that is a fierce turn of the screw. Boswell is held up to me as *the* model biographer from whom I must learn my craft. What would novelists say if I held up *Robinson Crusoe* as the supreme model for novelists?

Poeticus: *Robinson Crusoe* is a very fine story.

Plutarchus: Yes. And Boswell's *Johnson* is a very great biography. Moreover, I grant that Boswell himself, an extraordinary mixture of clown and reporter, kept admirable minutes, and knew how to find the vivid and the characteristic in the world around him. Everyone speaks of this biography as if it were the 'usual' and the model for the biographical art. It cannot be. Most biographers do not have the privilege of living close to their subjects for twenty years or more. And if Boswell was a fine reporter, he was the *worshipful* kind. The combination Boswell – Johnson worked. Such combinations are rare. The combination Thompson–Frost ran into trouble. Thompson wasn't worshipful; and then he knew Frost perhaps too long and too well. You wouldn't compare Joyce's biographer with Boswell: he never knew Joyce, and if he had known him, I think he would not have worshipped him as much. Nor can you compare Boswell with Painter who never knew Marcellus of France. Neither did Lord David Cecil know Melbourne, nor Edmund Wilson Lincoln, but Edmund's essay on Lincoln is extraordinary and Lord David's *Melbourne* is one of the great biographies of our time. You know, Criticus and Poeticus, I have toyed for years with the idea of writing an essay on modern Boswells: those who have tried and are trying to be Boswells. Archibald Henderson received a nod from Bernard Shaw but found G.B.S. too much for him. His book is as dull as Shaw was witty. The Thompson–Frost combination is particularly complex, a story of personal relations which a future biographer will have to unravel as part of Frost's life (and this is really true of Boswell and Johnson as well). One gathers that Frost wore on Thompson's nerves considerably, and the much praised candour which shows us the man behind the public figure and the poet will have to be examined for the buried feelings of the biographer. Is Thompson demolishing the poet by revealing the man who wore on his nerves? I think this a good question. Carvell Collins was to have been Faulkner's Boswell, but the writer's widow appointed someone else to do the authorized life; and something seems to be holding Collins back. Another complex problem of personal relations. Thornton Wilder appointed a Boswell, then changed his mind, and I can't discover whether this Boswell asked too many questions or failed in tact; but I know he ceased to receive encouragement. Boswellian biographies must be examined with care; and we must certainly look more closely at Lockhart and at Forster, who wrote out of intimate and long knowledge of their subjects. The *Life of Dr Johnson* is a very special case, like *Ulysses* or *Robinson Crusoe* in the novel. And it can teach little to a biographer who comes at a later stage, and works out of archives and memoirs, diaries and the author's writings. The poetics of biography, my dear Criticus, needs to be written you see, and by a biographer.

Criticus: It seems to me you've offered a very loose poetic. How would you sum up? Biographers are supposed to be good summarizers.

Plutarchus: I would begin with the idea that a life—the recreation in words of a life—is one of the most beautiful and most difficult tasks a literary artist can set himself. I would quote Lytton Strachey who said that human beings are too important to be treated as mere symptoms of the past. I would quote Henry James who said that a biography properly conceived and written can be 'one of the great observed adventures of mankind'. I would argue that telling the story of a life is not like telling any other story: certain things are given in advance, and that which is given must be weighed and discussed, perhaps as I've discussed *A Certain World*, but more thoroughly, of course, for I spoke off the cuff. Conjecture and speculation are required (what you might call the 'educated guess'), and the reader must be made aware of the guessing process as we are made aware of step-by-step procedures in a scientific experiment. Biographers encounter in our time prodigious archives, entire libraries. They must be discouraged from throwing segments of these archives at the reader, as if the archive were a formed life. The art of summary is indeed of supreme importance. Like Madame Curie, the biographer must melt down tons and tons of pitch-blende residues for many years, in order to arrive at a tiny glowing particle, the radium of human personality. Conrad once said, 'the dead can live only with the exact intensity of the life imparted to them by the living.' Having obtained his particle, the biographer must retain the glow, provide the intensity.

Criticus: Noble words, Plutarchus. But when you've melted down your materials, are you sure you haven't melted down much of the stuff of life? I don't want a biographer to give me digests and summaries, I want to read the documents for myself.

Plutarchus: Yes, I've heard that said very often. By all means, bury yourself in the archives; you will remain there for the rest of your life. As the poet distils his experience in a poem, and as the novelist should not be a photographer, so please permit the biographer to distil his work from his materials, and these are nowadays too abundant for anyone to read piecemeal and in their fragmented state. It's the biographer who takes the fragments and creates a mosaic, and his art resides in making you feel that you are creating it with him. He cross-examines himself about his choice of subject: why was he drawn to it? If he's honest with himself, he must inquire why he feels impelled to write about it. This is a psychological question, but until he has dealt with it he may find himself in a quandary, namely, that of believing that his subject can do no wrong. The drive to hero-worship is powerful, and there are few biographers who at the beginning are wholly disinterested. (We exclude always the hacks.) I could never write a biography of Hitler; I hate him too much, and besides I couldn't bear having to live with him for several years in the process. Biographies are written in love rather than hate, but it is a love in which the lover divests himself of his passion; the distortions of love fade; the subject becomes human, interesting, beautiful, ridiculous, odd, characteristic, original—a person who must be seen as he was, and not idealized. A biography is a kind of endless summary, in which the reader is made a party to a weighing of evidence.

Poeticus: And so you end where all poetics end. The poem derives from the poet; the biography derives from the biographer. You made up rules about pity and terror, the unities, the stuff of metrics, the rules of rhythm and rhyme, and you end up simply with artists making and finding.

Plutarchus: The poem derives from the poet; the biography derives from the biographer. Yes, Poeticus, but the poet derives from the biographer in rather important ways, and poets often forget this. I would ask poets and critics to remember poetry's harvest in the fields of my namesake, he who made parallels between the lives of noble Greeks and Romans. May it not be said that Plutarch set flowing, many centuries after he was dead, some of the greatest poetry we know, and the poet brought to life on the Elizabethan stage, and on all our stages since, old passions out of dead pages. It's a pretty question. What would Shakespeare's Romans have been without Plutarch, without all that ancient rumour, gossip, chronicle, old wives' tales which nevertheless embodied character, power, life and, as I say, passion? Plutarch chronicled and sketched his heroes thanks to an ideal of biography and a need to shore up, out of evanescence, the life that had been, even when it may only have been imagined. Biography and history became the vital bricks or cement or rough-hewn boards or what you will into which the supreme poet breathed his poetry. True, Plutarch wrote of war and action and dealt in the violence of life and the horror and pity of death, and not in literary biography. But I will not quibble; nor must you. Shakespeare could have made poetry of poets as well. He lent poetry to any life which he touched. But he had to have bricks as well as straw, and these were supplied by the vulgar superfluous fellow of Mr Auden's dictum.

Criticus: It's always easy to gild an argument with Shakespeare. Let us return to our theme. No poetics has ever lasted. No rules are ever devised for art that have not been derived from art.

Plutarchus: I suppose you would add that it is criticism that sets up the rules....

Criticus: No, I'm simply a reflecting mirror, a touchstone, the work is tested through me. I'm the reader's friend.

Poeticus: Critics are truly modest men.

Criticus: I don't like you, Poeticus.

Poeticus: That's why you are a critic.

Plutarchus: Come, the sunshine is turning lemon, but this is no excuse for the lemon in your voices. Let us complete this discussion at the high level at which we started. All that I can say is that a biographer must work by the illumination of his materials. He has no other guides. A single phrase may light up a whole chapter, which is why I never employ researchers. They wouldn't know which phrase to look at. I find it because my eye has been trained and my mind knows what's clutter and what's trivia, and what's significant detail. And then biographers have learned that all previous biographies must be turned topsy-turvy. For we know more about man's perverse fantasies and dream-logic, his ability to be rational about his irrationalities, and his extraordinary capacity to be imaginative in his self-delusion. We can no longer claim ourselves creatures of symmetry and logic. We are ambiguous and ambivalent; or if you find such words portentous, say we have mixed feelings. If we are prisoners of our genes and our environment we are also surrounded by unreliable witnesses, who see everything through the same imprisonment. The biographer Edelius told me something very interesting about his work on Henry James. He found that William James, the philosopher and older brother of Henry, is invariably quoted as a reliable witness to the life of his brother, even though that life was lived for almost half a century in the Old World away from William. Various critics have regarded as true William's reference to Henry as 'powerless-feeling', a statement which anyone who knows anything of his brother can recognize as untrue. Henry was a power-house, and his life was power-structured. He felt powerless only in the presence of his elder brother. Witnesses of lives are notoriously unreliable and the biographer must constantly be a cross-examining lawyer. The secret of Lytton Strachey's life was not his domestic arrangements with Carrington, poor troubled mischievous child-like woman, nor the men he loved, a history which fills two bulging volumes. The secret that requires an answer is why Lytton wrote about powerful women—Victoria, Elizabeth, Florence Nightingale—and usually ridiculed certain kinds of men. His choice of subjects and his handling of subjects, that is the real biography of Strachey, together with the other components of his art, his animus, his distortions, his prickliness. I am almost certain that Lytton Strachey not only identified himself with his own queen-like mother, so that he recreated Queens, but also felt he *was* his own mother, and thus mother of all the boys he loved. Carrington latched on to him for reasons that belong to *her* life. Lytton probably served as a father-brother to her. The biographer, you see, must look at everything. And while he feels his subject at certain moments, as if *he* were that subject, he detaches himself and uses his own eyes as well as those of the subject in order to arrive at his final picture. In a word, the new biography accepts the idea that there is a providence in every word a poet chooses, but it also knows it cannot always discover that providence.

Criticus: What you are saying is that a biography is tissued out of speculation; that is all it can be.

Poeticus: Do Plutarchus justice, Criticus. He often speculates on the firm ground of his author's choices. Lytton *did* write about Queens and was an old Queen himself! Wystan brought up the subject of vaginas and penises. And yet I'd hate to have you look into my life and speculate why I wear turtleneck sweaters.

Criticus: I always feel happier on critical ground than on biographical.

Plutarchus: Clearly. Confess, dear boy, that you're a disguised biographer. You review biographers, in your misguided way; you review volumes of letters. You show an insatiable interest in the personalities of the writers you deal with in your critical essays. So do all critics. They always cheat. They keep biographies hidden behind the books on their shelves or under counters. They say 'only the work'—no life, no biography. They say there is a 'biographical fallacy'. And then they perpetrate this very fallacy. I leave you again with the words of a poet who understood: I come back to Yeats. He said, 'We may come to think that nothing exists but a stream of souls, that all knowledge is biography.' How beautifully Yeats always cut through to a deep and essential truth!

The noon hour had long passed. The sun was buried behind London mists. The air had become chilly. The damp reasserted itself. The three figures became aware that they had been so engrossed in their discussion that a large part of the afternoon had evaporated. They knew how much time had gone by when the American Juno or Diana emerged and stood with her case and her papers on the steps hoping a taxi would come to deposit a reader and take her away.

Poeticus looked at her and said, 'How right you are, Plutarchus. I cannot think of her as a trap.'

Criticus assented. 'No woman so straight-limbed could be called a trap!'

Plutarchus laughed. 'I am a biographer,' he said. 'I can't be swayed by appearance as you are. I would have to investigate.'

Poeticus: You make biography sound a very sexy enterprise.

Plutarchus: Well, sex always helps. I'm sorry I've been so long-winded, but I feel I've offered a poetic, it has distilled itself from our talk. I wish we had a tape recorder.

In the background Tiresias switched off his tape recorder, from which I have taken this record.

Further Reading

Catherine Drinker Bowen, *Biography: The Craft and the Calling* (Boston), 1969.

James F. Clifford, *From Puzzles to Portraits* (Chapel Hill), 1970.

A. O. J. Cockshut, *Truth to Life: The Art of Biography in the 19th Century* (London), 1974.

Leon Edel, *Literary Biography* (London), 1957 & (Indiana Univ. Press), 1973.

John A. Garraty, *The Nature of Biography* (New York), 1967.

André Maurois, *Aspects de la Biographie* (Paris), 1927.

Harold Nicolson, *The Development of English Biography* (London), 1927.

James Olney, *Metaphors of the Self* (Princeton), 1972.

March Schorer, *The World We Imagine* (London), 1969.

Structuralism and Literature

JONATHAN CULLER

My main purpose here is to show that despite its more extreme manifestations structuralism is not an abstruse or recondite theory but that, on the contrary, a structuralist approach to literature is directly relevant to the practical study and teaching of literature. Further, I am going to assume from the first that the teaching of literature involves a concern with the fact that the objects of study are literary works rather than simply documents about inter-personal relations, and that students are supposed to learn about literature and how to read it, rather than about life and how to live.

There are, of course, good reasons for using literary works as ways of finding out about the possibilities of human experience: the images they offer are both more complex and less embarrassing to discuss than, say, another individual's account of relationships with parents or friends. And I think there would be much to be said from a structuralist or semiological point of view about the way in which attention of this kind tries to organize our world; but that is not what I am concerned with here. I shall assume that studying literature and teaching literature involve the development and mastery of special operations and procedures which are required for the reading of literature, as opposed to the reading of other kinds of texts.

First I shall try to explain what structuralism is and why it is especially relevant to the study of literature. Then I shall outline a structuralist approach to literature, both in general and with respect to several examples. But I should like to emphasize from the outset that I am not proposing a structuralist 'method' of interpretation: structuralism is not a new way of interpreting literary works, but an attempt to understand how it is that works do have meaning for us.

First, then, what is structuralism? Roland Barthes once defined it, in its 'most specialized and consequently most relevant version', as a method for the study of cultural artefacts derived from the methods of contemporary linguistics.[1] Now there are two possible ways of using linguistic methods in the study of literature. The first would be to describe in linguistic terms the language of literary texts. Many critics speak eloquently of the benefits of this approach, but it is not, I think, what Barthes meant by his definition nor is it the kind of structuralism with which I am concerned here. The second approach would be to take linguistics as a model which indicates how one might go about constructing a poetics which stands to literature as linguistics stands to language. In other words, one takes linguistics as an analogy which indicates how other cultural artefacts should be studied. For this kind of structuralism only a few fundamental principles of linguistics are directly relevant, of which the most important is Ferdinand Saussure's distinction between *langue* and *parole*.

La langue, the linguistic system, is what one knows when one knows English. *La parole*, specific utterances or speech acts, are instances of language, *la langue*. Saussure argued that *la langue*, the linguistic system, was the proper object of linguistics, and he went on to say that 'dans la langue il n'y a que des différences, sans termes positifs'. In the linguistic system there are only differences, with no positive terms. Study of *la langue* is an attempt to determine the nature of a system of relations, oppositions, and differences which makes possible *la parole*. In learning a language we master a linguistic system which makes actual communication possible, and the linguist's task is to describe and to make explicit what it is we have mastered.[2]

Taking this as a point of departure we can say that structuralism and its close relation semiology are based on two fundamental insights: first, that social and cultural phenomena do not have essences but are defined by a network of relations, both internal and external; and, secondly, that in so far as social and cultural phenomena, including literature, have meaning they are signs.

If one wished to distinguish between structuralism and semiology (and the reasons for the distinction are historical rather than logical), one could do so in these terms: structuralism studies the structures or systems of relations by which cultural

1. 'Science versus literature', *Times Literary Supplement*, 28 September 1967, p. 897.
2. See F. de Saussure, *Course in General Linguistics*, London, Fontana, 1974.

objects are defined and distinguished from one another; semiology studies cultural objects as signs that carry meanings. But I think that it is extremely important *not* to make the distinction, not to try to separate the two enterprises, since one entails the other where a profitable study of literature is concerned. If the two are separated one risks either discovering patterns of relations and oppositions which are irrelevant in that they have no sign function (this is the danger of the kind of linguistic analysis best represented by Roman Jakobson[3]), or else investigating signs on a one-to-one basis without due regard to the systems of convention which produce them (this is the danger of a limited semiological approach).

The task of structural analysis, we may then say, is to formulate the underlying systems of convention which enable cultural objects to have meaning for us. In this sense structuralism is not hermeneutic: it is not a method for producing new and startling interpretations of literary works (although in another sense which I shall mention below it *is* hermeneutic). It asks, rather, how the meanings of literary works are possible.

I should perhaps digress for a moment at this point to correct a frequent misapprehension about the relative status of literary theory and critical interpretation. It is common to speak of interpretations of particular works as though they were the central activity of literary criticism and to think of literary theory as something peripheral and altogether secondary, but of course the truth is quite the reverse. Interpretations of authors and works are wholly parasitic on the activity of reading literature: the critic who writes about an author is simply producing a more thorough and perhaps more perceptive version of what readers of literature do for themselves. But to enquire about the *nature* of literature, a theoretical task, is to ask what is involved in reading something *as* literature, and this is to tackle questions which are fundamental to anyone engaged in critical interpretation in that implicit answers are necessarily presupposed both by the activity of reading literature, and by the development of a discipline concerned with the study of literature as an institution.

The best way to ease oneself into this structuralist perspective is to take linguistics as a model and to think of the relationship

---

3. See Roman Jakobson, *Questions de poétique*, Paris, Seuil, 1973. For discussion see Culler, *Structuralist Poetics*, chapter III.

between an utterance and the speaker/hearer. A sentence which I utter comes to you as a series of physical events, a sequence of sounds which we might represent by a phonetic transcription. You hear this sequence of sounds and give it a meaning. The question linguistics asks is how is this possible, and the answer, of course, is that you bring to the act of communication an immense amount of implicit, subconscious knowledge. You have assimilated the phonological system of English which enables you to relate these physical sounds to the abstract and relational phonemes of English; you have assimilated a grammatical system, so complex that we are only beginning to understand it, which enables you to assign a structural description to the sentence, to ascertain the relations among its parts, and to recognize it as grammatically well-formed, even though you have never heard it before; and finally, your knowledge of the semantic component of the language enables you to assign an interpretation to this string of sounds. Now we may say, if we wish, that the phonological and syntactic structure and the meaning are *properties* of the utterance, so long as we remember that they are properties of the utterance only with respect to the complex grammar which speakers of English have assimilated. Without the complex knowledge brought to the communicative act, they have none of these properties.

Moving from language to literature, we find an analogous situation. Imagine someone who knows English but has no knowledge of literature and indeed no acquaintance with the concept of literature. If presented with a poem he would be quite baffled. He would understand words and sentences, certainly, but he would not know what this strange thing was; he would not, quite literally, know what to do with this curious linguistic construction. What he lacks is a complex system of knowledge that experienced readers have acquired, a system of conventions and norms which we might call 'literary competence'. And we can say that just as the task of linguistics is to make explicit the system of a language which makes linguistic communication possible, so in the case of literature a structuralist poetics must enquire what knowledge must be postulated to account for our ability to read and understand literary works.

Lest you be sceptical about the importance of this implicit knowledge that we bring to the act of reading poetry, let me offer a simple and crude example. Take a perfectly ordinary sentence, such as 'Yesterday I went into town and bought a lamp', and set it down on a page as a poem:

> Yesterday I
> Went into town and bought
> A lamp.

The words remain the same, and if meanings change it is because we approach the poem with different expectations and interpretative operations. What sort of thing happens? First of all, 'Yesterday' takes on a different force: it no longer refers to a particular day but to the set of possible yesterdays and serves primarily to set up a temporal opposition within the poem (between present and recent past). This is due to our conventions about the relationship of poems to the moment of utterance. Secondly, we expect the lyric to capture a moment of some significance, to be thematically viable; and we thus apply to 'lamp' and 'bought' conventions of symbolic extrapolation. The traditional associations of *lamp* are obvious; *buying* we can take as one mode of acquisition as opposed to others; and we thus acquire potential thematic material. Thirdly, we expect a poem to be a unified whole and thus we must attempt to interpret the fact that this poem ends so swiftly and inconclusively. The silence at the end can be read as a kind of ironic comment, a blank, and we can set up an opposition between the action of buying a lamp, the attempt to acquire light, and the failure to tell of any positive benefits which result from yesterday's action. This general structure can, of course, support a variety of paraphrases, but any interpretation of the poem is likely to make use of these three elementary operations enshrined in the institution of poetry. The conventions of the lyric create the possibility of new and supplementary meanings.

Note also, and this is important, that though in one sense these meanings are in the poem—they are public, can be argued about, and do not depend upon individual subjective associations—in another sense, which is more important given the current critical climate, they are not *in* the poem. They depend on operations performed by readers (and assumed by poets).

Though this may seem obvious, there are good reasons for insisting on it. What we still call the New Criticism, in its desire to free the text from a controlling authorial intention, wanted to convince us that meanings could be there in the language of the text. The poem was to be thought of as complete in itself, a harmonious totality, not unlike an autonomous self-sufficient natural organism. Despite the salutary effects of this Coleridgean line of criticism, which I should not in the least want to deny, it was perhaps inevitable that it should lead to the notion that the critic or reader, like a good empiricist, approaches the poem without preconceptions and attempts to appreciate fully what is there. Such a notion leads to a theoretical impasse, to a hopeless attempt to show how the language of poetry itself differs from the language of prose or everyday speech.

Structuralism leads us to think of the poem not as a self-contained organism but as a sequence which has meaning only in relation to a literary system, or rather, to the 'institution' of literature which guides the reader. The sense of a poem's completeness is a function of the totality of the interpretive process, the result of the way we have been taught to read poems. And to avoid misunderstanding I should perhaps emphasize that, though it is preferable to talk about reading rather than writing, we are dealing with conventions which are assumed by the writer. He is not just setting words down on paper but writing a poem. Even when he is in revolt against the tradition, he still knows what is involved in reading and writing poems; and when he chooses among alternative words or phrases, he does so as a master of reading.

Although this notion of a literary system or of literary competence may be anathema to many, the reasons which lead one to postulate it are quite convincing. First of all, the claims of schools and universities to offer literary training cannot be lightly dismissed: it is, alas, only too clear that knowledge of English and a certain experience of the world do not suffice to make someone a perceptive reader of literature. Something else is required, something which literary training is designed to provide. And a poetics ought to be able to go some way towards specifying what is supposed to be learned. We presume, after all, to judge a student's progress towards literary competence: our examinations are not designed merely to check whether he or she has read and remembered certain books but to test his or her progress as a reader of literature. And that presumption suggests that there is something to be learnt here.

Secondly, it seems obvious that the study of one work facilitates the study of the next. We gain not only points of comparison but a sense of how to read—general formal principles and distinctions that have proved useful, questions which one addresses to certain kinds of texts, a sense of what one is looking for. We can speak if we like of extrapolating from one work to another, so long as we do not thereby obscure the fact that it is precisely this extrapolation which requires explanation. If we are to make any sense of the process of literary education we must assume, as Northrop Frye says, the possibility of 'a coherent and comprehensive theory of literature . . . some of which the student unconsciously learns as he goes along, but the main principles of which are as yet unknown to us.'[4]

What are the obstacles to this kind of enterprise? First, critics are accustomed to think of their task as that of producing new and subtler interpretations of literary works, and to ask them to attend to what must be taken for granted by experienced readers of literature cannot but seem an impoverishment of the critical enterprise. Just as most people are more interested in using their language than in trying to determine the nature of their linguistic competence, so most critics are more interested in exercising their understanding of literature than in investigating what it involves. But of course in the first case we do not deceive ourselves that those engaged in using their linguistic competence are thereby participating in the study of language, whereas in the second case critics have succeeded in making us believe that their discussion of individual works constitutes the study of literature. This notion is a significant obstacle; but if we are at all concerned with the nature of literature itself, and if we recognize the desirability of understanding what it is that we expect our students to learn, we would do well to grant poetics its proper status at the centre of literary studies.

The second obstacle seems more serious: the difficulty of determining what will count as evidence for literary competence, evidence about the assumptions and operations of reading. It might seem that critics differ so widely in their interpretations as to undermine any notion of a general literary competence. But I should stress first of all that this is not, in fact, an obstacle which must be overcome initially, but a matter which will resolve itself in practice. Since what one is trying to do is to determine the conventions and operations which will

---

4. *Anatomy of Criticism*, New York, Atheneum, 1965, p. 11.

account for certain effects, one begins by specifying what effects in fact one is attempting to explain, and then constructs models to account for them. As it is obvious that there is a range of acceptable readings for any poem, what one attempts to discover are the operations which account for this range of readings. In the case of the brief poem which I discussed above, I assumed that the sentence had different possible meanings when set down as a poem rather than as a prose statement, and offered some crude hypotheses to explain why this should be so. If you think that it is not so, if the meanings do not strike you as acceptable in terms of your own literary competence, you will reject the hypotheses and the explanation as false. The only danger, in other words, is that you will find what I have to say irrelevant because I am trying to account for facts which you do not accept. However, even if one were to succeed only in describing in an explicit fashion one's own literary competence, that would be a significant achievement. And because literary competence is the result of an interpersonal experience of reading and discussion, any account of it will doubtless cover much common ground.

Moreover it cannot be emphasized too strongly that some kind of literary competence is presupposed by everyone who discusses or writes about literature. Any critic who claims to offer more than a purely personal and idiosyncratic response to a text is claiming that his interpretation derives from operations of reading that are generally accepted, that it is possible to convince readers of its validity because there are shared points of departure and common notions of how to read, and that both critic and audience know what counts as evidence for a reading, what can be taken for granted, and what must be explicitly argued for. What I am asking is that we try to grasp more clearly this common basis of reading and thus to make explicit the conventions which make literature possible.

A structuralist approach starts by stressing the artificiality of literature, the fact that though literature may be written in the language of information it is not used in the 'language-game' of giving information. It is obvious, for example, that by convention the relationship of speaker to utterance is different when we are dealing with a poem and with another speech act. The poet does not stand in the same relation to a lyric as to a letter he has written, even if the poem be Ben Jonson's 'Inviting a Friend to Supper'. This initial strangeness, this artifice, is the primary fact with which we have to deal, and we can say that the techniques of reading are ways of simultaneously cherishing and overcoming this strangeness—ways of 'naturalizing' the text and making it something of a communication. To naturalize a text—I use this word in preference to what some of the French theorists call *vraisemblablisation*—is to transform it so that it can be assimilated to an order of *vraisemblance*. This is absolutely basic to the reading of literature, and a simple example would be the interpretation of metaphor. When Shelley writes 'my soul in an enchanted boat' we must, in order to 'understand' this, naturalize the figure; we must perform a semantic transformation on 'enchanted boat' so as to bring it under a particular order of *vraisemblance*, which here we might call 'possible characteristics of the soul'. Of course, the fact that understanding involves more than translation of this kind must be stressed: we must preserve the distance traversed in the act of translation as a sign in its own right. Here, for example, we have a sign of a particular lyric posture, of the poetical character, of the inadequacy of ordinary discourse, and so on.

Now there are various levels at which we can naturalize, various sets of conventions which can be brought into play. And of course these change with the institution of literature itself, so that once a style or mode of discourse becomes established it is possible to naturalize a poem as a comment upon this literary mode. When we read Lewis Carroll's 'A-Sitting on a Gate' as a parody of Wordsworth's 'Resolution and Independence' we naturalize the former and make its strange features intelligible as commentary upon the latter.

The conventions of literature guide the process of naturalization and provide alternatives to what might be called 'premature naturalization'. This is a direct move from poem to utterance which ignores the former's specifically literary characteristics, as if we were to naturalize Donne's 'The Good Morrow' by saying: the poet was in bed with his mistress one morning when the sun rose and, being still befuddled with drink, he uttered this statement in the hope that the sun would go away and shine elsewhere. If one had no knowledge of the institution of literature this is what one might be tempted to do, but even the least advanced student knows that this is an inappropriate step, that he must naturalize at another level which takes into account some of the conventions of literature. The protest to the sun is itself a figure; the situation of the utterance of a poem is a fiction which must be incorporated in our interpretation. We are likely to naturalize 'The Good Morrow' as a love poem which uses this situation as an image of energy and annoyance, and hence as a figure for a strong, self-sufficient passion.

This ought at least to indicate what I mean by naturalization: it is the process of making something intelligible by relating it to what is already known and accepted as *vraisemblable*. We are guided in this process by various codes of expectations which we ought to try to make explicit. In discussing prose fiction Roland Barthes identifies five different codes, but I shall mention just two by way of example.[5]

What Barthes calls the semic code is an especially good case of literary conventions which produce intelligibility. As we go through a novel we pick out items which refer to the behaviour of characters and use them, as we say, to create character. Generally this involves considerable semantic transformation. Cultural stereotypes enable us to move from descriptions of dress or behaviour to qualities of persons, and we admit in fiction moves which we would not accept in ordinary circumstances. We do not believe that there is a real correlation between perfect or blemished complexions and perfect or blemished moral character, but certain *genres* permit inferences of this kind. We do not believe that blonde women as a class have different qualities from brunettes as a class, but the conventions of literature provide us with a set of opposed qualities with which the opposition between a blonde and a dark heroine may be correlated. Indeed, in order to see literature as an agent of moral education, as Christopher Butler has urged, we have to assume that literature will provide us with models of personality and ways of relating action to motive which are not the fruit of our ordinary experience; one of the things a reader of literature learns, that is to say, is how to construct personalities out of the notations that the text offers. He acquires mastery of the semic code.

The symbolic code is one of the oddest and most difficult to

---

5. Roland Barthes, *S/Z*, see Further Reading, p. 76.

discuss. It is also the code with which students have the greatest difficulty, and both students and teachers ought to attempt to gain clearer notions of what it involves than we have at present. What governs the perception and interpretation of symbols? There are obviously a few symbols, consecrated by tradition, which seem to bear an intrinsic meaning, but most potential symbols are defined by complex relations with a context. The rose, for example, can lead in a variety of directions, and within each of these semantic fields (religion, love, nature) its significance will depend on its place in an oppositional structure. Sun and moon can signify almost anything, provided the opposition between them is preserved. Although, as I say, this code is poorly understood, it seems clear that symbolic extrapolation is a teleological process with a set of goals which limit the range of plausible interpretations and specify what kind of meanings serve as adequate *terminii and quem* For example, there is a rule of generalization: to be told that in a phrase like 'shine on my bowed head, O moon' the moon symbolizes 'the quarterly production quota set by the district manager' is bathetic. We quickly learn that there is a set of semantic oppositions, such as life and death, simplicity and complexity, harmony and strife, reality and appearance, body and soul, certainty and doubt, imagination and intellect, which are culturally marked as in some way 'ultimate' and hence as goals in the process of symbolic extrapolation. But we ought to be able to say a good deal more about this process which we expect students to master.

After these sketchy indications of the problems involved, I should like to turn by way of example to the kind of fundamental expectations concerning poetry which govern the operation of codes and the process of naturalization. We might start with a short poem by William Carlos Williams:

> This is Just to Say
>
> I have eaten
> the plums
> that were in
> the icebox
>
> and which
> you were probably
> saving
> for breakfast

Forgive me
they were delicious
so sweet
so cold

The fact that this is printed on a page as a poem brings into play our expectations concerning poetry (as sentences in a novel it would, of course, be read differently), the first of which we might call the convention of distance and impersonality. Although at one level the sentences are presented as a note asking forgiveness for eating plums, since poetry is by convention detached from immediate circumstances of utterance we deprive it of this pragmatic function, retaining simply the reference to a context as an implicit statement that this kind of experience is important, worthy of poetry. By doing this we avoid the premature naturalization which says, 'the poet ate the plums and left this note on the table for his wife, writing it as verse because he was a poet'.

Starting then with the assumption that this is not a pragmatic utterance but a lyric in which a fictional 'I' speaks of eating plums, we are faced with the question of what to do with this object, how to structure it. We expect poems to be organic wholes and we possess a variety of models of wholeness: the simplest is the binary opposition which is given a temporal dimension (not X but Y); another is the unresolved opposition (neither X nor Y but both simultaneously); next there is the dialectical resolution of a binary opposition; and finally, remaining with simple models of wholeness, the four-term homology (X is to Y as A is to B) or the series closed and summed up by a transcendent final term. In studying this poem we need to apply a model of completeness so as to secure an opening up of the poem and to establish a thematic structure into which we can fit its elements, which thus become sets of features subject to thematic expansion. Our elementary model of the opposition can here take the thematic form of rule and transgression: the plums were to be saved for breakfast but they have been eaten. We can then group various features on one side or the other: on the side of 'eating' we have 'delicious', 'sweet' and 'cold', stressed by their final position (this is a conventional rule) and implying that eating plums was indeed worth it; on the other side we have the assumed priority of domestic rules about eating (one recognizes them and asks for forgiveness), the reference to 'breakfast', the orderly life represented by the hypostatization of meal-times. The process of thematic interpretation requires us to move from facts towards values, so we can develop each thematic complex, retaining the opposition between them. Thus we have the valuing of immediate sensuous experience, as against an economy of order and saving, which is also valued, though transgressed.

Then, presumably, the question we must ask ourselves is whether this structure is complete: whether the opposition is a simple one, a move from X to Y, or whether the attitude of the poem is in fact more complex and requires us to call upon other models. And here we can take account of what we earlier set aside—the fact that the poem masquerades as a note asking forgiveness. We can say that the poem itself acts as a mediating force, recognizing the priority of conventions (by the act of writing a note) but also seeking absolution. We can also give a function at this level to the deictics, the 'I' and 'you' which we had set aside, taking the relationship as a figure of intimacy, and say that the note tries to bring this realm of immediate sensuous experience into the realm of interpersonal relations, where there will be tension, certainly, but where (as the abrupt ending of the poem implies) there is hope that intimacy and understanding will resolve the tension.

Although I have been naming and paraphrasing, what I am producing is, of course, a thematic structure which could be stated in various ways. The claim is simply that in interpreting a poem like this we are implicitly relying on assumptions about poetry and structural models without which we could not proceed: that our readings of the poem (which will, of course, differ) depend upon some common interpretive operations.

Interpretation might generally stop here, but if we think about the fact that these sentences are presented as a poem we can go a step further by asking 'why?'. Why should this sort of banal statement be a poem? And here, by an elementary reversal which is crucial to the reading of modern poetry, we can take banality of statement as a statement about banality and say that the world of notes and breakfast is also the world of language, which must try to make a place for this kind of immediate experience which sounds banal and whose value can only be hinted at. This, we could go on to say, is why the poem must be so sparse and apparently incomplete. It must produce, as it were, a felt absence, a sense of missing intensity and profundity, so that in our desire to read the poem and to make it complete we will supply what the poem itself dare not claim: the sense of significance.

Let me turn now to a poem of a rather different kind, one which is usually read as a political statement and act of engagement, Blake's 'London'.

> I wander through each chartered street,
> Near where the chartered Thames does flow,
> And mark in every face I meet
> Marks of weakness, marks of woe.
>
> In every cry of every Man,
> In every Infant's cry of fear,
> In every voice, in every ban,
> The mind-forged manacles I hear.
>
> How the Chimney-sweeper's cry
> Every black'ning Church appalls;
> And the hapless Soldier's sigh
> Runs in blood down Palace walls.
>
> But most thro' midnight streets I hear
> How the youthful Harlot's curse
> Blasts the new-born Infant's tear,
> And blights with plagues the Marriage hearse.

I don't want to suggest that this isn't a political poem, but I would like to impress upon you how much work we must do in order to make it a political statement and what a variety of extremely artificial conventions we must call upon in order to read it in this way.

The poem is organized as a list of things seen and heard: I mark marks; I hear manacles; I hear how.... And it is obvious from the outset that the things heard or seen are bad (marks of weakness, marks of woe, manacles, blasts and blights). This gives us our initial opposition between the perceiving subject and the objects of perception and provides a thematic centre which helps us to organize details. We may start with the assumption, based on the convention of unity, that we have a series which will cohere at some level (the second stanza with its repetitions of 'every' is ample warrant for that).

But it is quite difficult to produce this coherence. In the third stanza we can try to collate the two propositions in order to discover their common subject: I hear how the cry of the sweep and the sigh of the soldier act upon the church or palace. This gives us a sound (which fits into the series of 'marks' which the 'I' perceives), an actor (who, our cultural model tells us, counts among the oppressed), and an institution which they affect. The opposition between institution and oppressed is one whose parameter we know: the possibilities are those of protest and submission, the results the indifference or guilt of the institution. And in fact the structure which Blake has established is ambiguous enough to preclude our really knowing which to choose here. One critic, citing historical evidence, argues that the sigh of the soldier is the murmur of possible rebellion and that the visionary can already see the blood on palace walls in a native version of the French Revolution. But we can also say, in an alternative naturalization, that the palace is bloody because it is responsible for the blood of soldiers whom it commands. Both readings, of course, are at some distance from the 'sigh running in blood', but we are sufficiently accustomed to such interpretive operations for this not to worry us.

What, though, of the chimney-sweep? One might assume that the Church is horrified ('appalled') at the conditions of child labour, but the convention of coherence invariably leads critics to reject this reading and to emphasize that 'appall' means to make pale or (since by convention puns are permitted when relevant) to cast a pall over and to weaken the Church's moral authority. The 'black'ning' church either becomes black, with guilt as well as soot, or makes things black by its indifference and hypocrisy; and the cry of the sweep changes its colour either by making it pale or by casting a pall of metaphorical soot over it. Our ability to perform these acts of semantic transference, moving 'black' and 'soot' around from sweep to church to its moral character, works as a kind of proof of the poem, a demonstration that there is a rich logical coherence and semantic solidarity here. The point, however, is that the lines do not carry an obvious meaning; they cannot be naturalized as an intimation of oppression without the help of a considerable amount of condensation and displacement.

The last stanza too has an intial strangeness which is difficult to naturalize. The speaker hears how a harlot's curse blasts a tear. We could, of course, read this as a harlot cursing at the fact that her own baby is crying, but since this is to be the climax of the poem we are constrained to reject this interpretation as premature naturalization. Indeed, such is the force of conventional expectations that no commentary I have read cites this reading, though it is the most obvious. To produce unity we must discover mind-forged manacles, and the best candidate for manacling is the infant. If we are to allow his tear to be blasted we must perform semantic operations on it: the tear can be an expression of protest and feeling, of innocence also perhaps, which is cursed and manacled not so much by the curse of the harlot (and again we become involved in semantic transfers) as by her existence. Her curse becomes her sign or mark and thus fits into the series of sounds which the narrator hears. By another transfer we can say that the infant himself is cursed, as he becomes an inhabitant of this world of harlots and charters. Similarly, in the last line we can transfer epithets to say that it is marriage itself which is blighted, so that the wedding carriage becomes a hearse, through the existence of the harlot. We could, of course, work out a casual relationship here (marriage is weakened if husbands visit harlots), but the level of generality at which the poem operates suggests that this will make coherence difficult. 'London' is not after all a description of specific social evils, and that, if we read the poem as a protest, is a fact with which we must now contend.

We must ask, in other words, what we are to say about the fact that the poem goes some way towards defeating our expectations: the cries are not cries of misery only but every cry of every man, even the shouts of street vendors. What are we to make, shall we say, of this odd semiotic procedure and of the interpretive requirements which the poem imposes upon us? There is a great distance which the reader must traverse in order to get from the language of the text to political protest. What does this signify? And the answer is, I think, that here, in the kind of reading which the poem requires, we have a representation of the problems of the visionary state. The distance between every cry and mind-forged manacles is great, so great that there is a possible ambiguity about whose mind is manacled. The speaker 'marks marks'; is it because he is 'marking' that he sees marks? He perceives, after all, the same thing in every street cry, in every face. In order to make sense of this we must construct an identity for the 'I' of the poem; we must postulate the figure of a visionary who sees what no one else sees, who can traverse these distances and read signs whose meaning is obscure to other observers. The city is not itself aware of its problems, its grief. The gap between appearance and awareness is presented, we can say, as the greatest terror of London. The true misery of manacles forged in the mind lies in the fact that they restrict the perception of misery and that no one else, not even the reader until the poem has forced him to exercise his symbolic imagination, can see the blood run down palace walls.

This has been a laboured account of what seems required if we are to read the poem as we do. It is not a structuralist interpretation for it agrees, except for the last paragraph, with customary readings of the poem. If it seems different, that is because it tries to make explicit some of the operations which we are accustomed to taking for granted. Some of these operations are highly conventional; they involve a special logic of literary interpretation, and it is not at all strange that critics prefer to take them for granted. But I think that if we are concerned with the nature of literature itself, or with dispelling the popular notion of the interpretation of literary texts as involving a complex guessing game, it is important to think more explicitly about the operations which our interpretations presuppose.

I think also, and my final remarks on 'London' were designed to provide some hint of this, that the last stage in our interpretation of a poem ought to be one which returns dialectically to its source, which takes into consideration the kind of naturalization and the interpretive conventions which the poem has compelled us to use, and which asks what these demands signify. For finally the meaning of a poem will lie in the kinds of operations which it forces us to perform, in the extent to which it resists or complies with our expectations about literary signs. It is in this sense that the structuralist poetics can be hermeneutic. If we become accustomed to thinking of literature as a set of interpretive norms and operations, we will be better equipped to see (and this is crucial in the case of the most modern and difficult texts) how and where the work resists us, and how it leads to that questioning of the self and of received modes of ordering the world which has always been the result of the greatest literature.

My readers, says the narrator at the end of *A la recherche du temps perdu*, will become 'les propres lecteurs d'eux-mêmes'. In my book, he says, they will read themselves and their own limits. How better to facilitate a reading of the self than by gaining a sense of the conventions of intelligibility that define the self, than by trying to make explicit one's sense of order and disorder, of the significant and the insignificant, of the naturalized and the bizarre? In its resolute artificiality, literature challenges the limits we set to the self as an agent of order and allows us to accede, painfully or joyfully, to an expansion of self. But that requires, if it is to be fully accomplished, a measure of awareness of the modes of ordering which are the components of one's culture, and it is for that reason that I think a structuralist poetics has a crucial role to play, not only in advancing an understanding of literature as an institution but also in promoting the richest experience of reading.

Further Reading

Roland Barthes, *S/Z* (Paris, Seuil), 1970. *Critique et vérité* (part II), (Paris, Seuil), 1966. 'Introduction à l'analyse structurale des récits', *Communications* 8, 1966.

Jonathan Culler, *Structuralist Poetics* (London, Routledge, and Cornell Univ. Press), 1975. *Flaubert, The Uses of Uncertainty* (London, Elek, and Cornell Univ. Press), 1974.

Gérard Genette, *Figures II* (Paris, Seuil), 1969.

Stephen Heath, *The Nouveau Roman* (London, Elek), 1972.

Barbara H. Smith, *Poetic Closure* (Chicago University Press), 1968.

Tzvetan Todorov, *La Poétique*, revised edition, Collection Points (Paris, Seuil), 1973.

Tragedy and Moral Education

CHRISTOPHER BUTLER

The essay which follows may need some introduction. In it I try to show how literature in general and tragedy in particular has profound moral effects provided we accept that literature throws light on the way we see the world and the beliefs we entertain about it. Furthermore, if we are to see these effects as being not only moral but also educative, we ought at the outset to have some idea of what a morally educated person would be like, in order to be able to estimate what would count as morally educative success.

I am going to assume that such persons, whatever general beliefs or principles of action they may have, are at least able to fulfill the following four requirements: (i) to identify with other persons in such a way that *their* beliefs or points of view are taken account of; (ii) to be aware of and have insight into their own and other people's feelings; (iii) to master relevant factual knowledge (for example, that sort of knowledge which shows how 'circumstances alter cases'); (iv) to exercise the three abilities above in evolving those moral principles which help them to make moral judgements.[1]

My argument from here is in essence very simple. It is that literature by its very nature provides us with a uniquely valuable exercise of these abilities. Literature makes us go through mental processes which are just those required for moral insight. I am in fact trying to give a clearer specification of Shelley's claim in his *Defence of Poetry* that 'the primary instrument of moral good is the imagination; and poetry administers to the effect by acting on the cause'. (In trying to show this I rely

---

1. I draw these assumptions from J. Wilson, G. Williams and B. Sugarman, *An Introduction to Moral Education*, Penguin, 1968, especially pp. 192ff.; also from C. Butler, 'Literature and Moral Education' in *Moral Education* Vol. 1, No. 1, 1969.

upon examples drawn from tragedy, but I hope that my argument can apply to any of the *genres*.)

However, one may well wish to avoid any such considerations as referred to above by arguing that moral questions may be thought to trespass illicitly into areas essentially private. Such attempts to avoid moral considerations when dealing with literature would have a good practical basis, quite apart from any wish to flee from the legally and politically tangled question of censorship. For literature's moral effects may be indeed a largely *empirical* matter which lies well outside a mere concern for the elucidation of literary works. This is partly because these moral effects may be most pronounced when observed as tied to differences in culture. Yet as literary critics rather than sociologists we (pre)tend to deal with a culture unified by literary tradition, and an awareness of the continuous history of ideas amongst other things, which is supposed to be the possession of the 'educated'. One has only to add the admittedly insidious assumption that the 'educated' are morally robust, and the consequence is that the literary critic then fails to deal with just those works (and audiences) which are associated with the most socially widespread moral effects.

For instance, we may assume that literature can typically evoke an 'empathic response'. Now this response as it affects subsequent behaviour may be considerably more pronounced and important in the case of the audience for Mickey Spillane, than it is for the audience for *King Lear*, Genêt, or the 'theatre of cruelty'. Thus the proviso needs to be made at the outset, that if we were to study the *formation* of moral beliefs by reading, we would probably have to study texts rather different from those we normally do, and would in any case be in some confusion about the relationship between 'reading' and other sources of moral development.

Similar problems arise for morally biased 'cultural diagnosis' of a general kind such as is practised by critics like Lionel Trilling, Morse Peckham, Northrop Frye, Marshall McLuhan, and by Arnold of course before them. For it is a matter of *empirical* fact, best pursued in the behavioural sciences, to decide whether poetry has taken the place of religion as Arnold prophesied, or whether literary people are 'better at morals/human relationships' than scientists, or whether it was true in 1962, that, in Graham Hough's words, few of the pupils of English teachers 'have read any Dickens, none has read any Scott, but every-body has read *Franny and Zooey* and *The Loneliness of the Long Distance Runner*, two books extremely removed from the lives these young people actually live but seductive because they embody one of the current religious substitutes—the myth of the juvenile saviour, the tragic dying god.'[2] This very Arnoldian remark incorporates an interesting psychological assumption which we shall discuss below.

However, the moral significance of literature must be faced at some point, just as its ideological significance has to be: one cannot indefinitely say 'that's an empirical matter and we don't know the answer yet'. Without *some* theoretical discussion we would not know the direction in which to look in any case. It is indeed difficult to cite major works of literature which are not generally taken to have some moral significance, and it thus becomes impossible to specify a satisfactory set of critical principles which are independent of moral considerations, in so far as grasping the significance of a work is not a neutrally intellectual process, but can modify our subsequent behaviour. (One must not, however, run the risk of making a training in critical appreciation the occasion of covert moral education, any more than of political education.) For there is a sense in which literature may provide us not simply with the free play of mental processes, but also with *knowledge* that may engage our sense of responsibility for states of affairs, and thus ultimately our responsibility for moral action.

By and large we *know* what our moral principles are (or should be) and do not need to be *taught* them by literature. For moral principles and beliefs lie within a central (if very problematic) core of our human thinking in a way that, for example, scientific theories or political and religious ideologies do not. (Thus incidentally, those who wish to interfere with literature for its supposedly corrupting effects, are generally confessing their inability to teach morals at the proper stage and in the proper place—in the church, in the family, in society at large, or wherever they prefer. For the understanding of works of literature often goes far beyond the level at which one is morally defenceless.) If it is assumed that people are neither physically assaulted by books nor taught their religion by them, then the

---

2. Graham Hough, *The Dream and the Task*, 1963, p. 23. The subtitle of this book is 'Literature and Morals in the Culture of Today'.

serious artist can often be seen as merely calling into question moral beliefs against some relatively settled background of belief, or the lack of it, in his society. He does not coerce moral action.

Nevertheless it is when generally accepted moral conventions are in tension with literature that the situation becomes *critically* interesting. Thus it is the complexity (and perhaps resolution) of a moral *problem* that most frequently is able to carry with it its proper artistic form (as, for example, Wallace Stevens's 'Sunday Morning' and Henry James's *The Golden Bowl*). And it is the writer who can show us most clearly the elements in such problems—conflict between characters, significant choices, the consequences of actions, and so on all within the ordered time structure of his plots. Thus I am much in sympathy with Chekhov, when he writes to Suvorin:

> You are right in demanding that the artist should take a conscious [moral] attitude to his work, but you confuse two conceptions. *The solution of a question and the correct setting of a question.* The latter alone is obligatory for an artist. In *Anna Karenina* and *Onegin* not a single problem is solved, but they satisfy completely because all the problems are set correctly. It is for the judge to set the questions correctly: and the young men must decide, each according to his taste.[3]

Thus in the *Oresteia*, one of the earliest of tragedies, a main theme, commented on by the chorus, is that:

> the impious act
> begets more after it,
> like to the stock from whence they come.
> (*Agamemnon*, 758–60)

This both raises a moral problem and calls forth a dramatic structure for the subsequent two plays, as well as casting our minds back beyond the *Agamemnon*. For, once Thyestes has eaten his own children and cursed the house of Atreus, a dialectic of conflict is set up that, as the very structure of the trilogy shows, can only resolve itself by working in the direction of an impartial justice. But the real problem lies in seeing how any

---

3. Anton Pavelovich Chekhov, letter to A. S. Suvorin, 27 October 1888, in *Selected Letters*, tr. S. Lederer, ed. L. Hellman, 1955, p. 57.

act of justice can be introduced. For, as Professor Kitto remarks:

> we can [at the end of *Agamemnon*] see that *all* the crimes this house has known and will know are of the same pattern, all of them are acts of 'justice' that will know no end. Clytemnaestra [before killing Agamemnon] prays to Zeus Teleios, Zeus the Achiever, but here is no sign of finality, nor can there be.[4]

Thus critics have had great difficulty in seeing how the formal introduction of Athenian justice in the last play actually resolves the moral problem and pattern of action of the two preceding. There is a tension of ideologies between the central characters (ultimately Orestes), the gods (through the Furies), and Athenian justice. There can be little doubt though that Aeschylus has set up an exceedingly difficult problem, and that it is up to us in interpreting the trilogy to ask questions about the moral, philosophical, and indeed political validity of the formal solution.[5]

But there is a further matter which I would like to raise at this stage. This is comprised in the assertion that literature may not only be distinctive in setting moral problems, but also may help us to have appropriate emotions in morally significant situations. If the improvement and clarification of feeling is as essential an element in moral education as the inculcation of right choices, that is, if our concept of intentionally performed moral acts requires something *more* than the mere following of a moral principle, then one possible line of defence for literary studies as a whole seems to be that they do 'educate the emotions' in a way that may provide some of these extra components in our moral actions.

Thus we could, for example, view the Romantic movement or the eighteenth-century concern with 'sublimity' in part as attempts to teach us to attach emotions to particular situations and objects, and in so doing extend our range of responses, using rhetorical techniques to increase the intensity of the emotion felt. (We could, for example, see the poetry of the First World War in this light. As the war dragged on, poets were not simply

4. H. D. F. Kitto, *Form and Meaning in Drama*, Methuen, 1956, 1960, p. 51.
5. For a further discussion of this, see Hugh Lloyd Jones, *The Justice of Zeus*, Berkeley, Los Angeles and London, 1971, pp. 90–95.

drawing attention to different *things*, but also re-educating their public emotionally, by getting them to see what Owen called the 'pity' of war rather than its martial glory. The nature of the violence in the poetry changes, from the flashing of metaphorical swords, to the blood 'gargling from the froth of corrupted lungs' of a dying soldier.) In an important sense then, literature may educate the emotions in getting its audience to attach emotions to 'proper' objects, by working on the audience's beliefs *and* emotional attitudes by means of the concrete presentation of these objects, persons and situations.

But it is not so much emotions and objects as emotions and persons that are most significant here. We thus need to extend our argument. The premise here is that it is essential to our potential for moral action that we should have a concept of human character; and also, that in consequence of this concept we should be able to let the interests of other people as they appear to *them* weigh with us. Now as we follow through the dramatic situations of a novel or play or poem, we are released from our single point of view, and are given the illusion of seeing the events from the point of view of another person or persons. (The novel, as Henry James was at some pains to make clear, manipulates the reader very deliberately in this respect.) If one of the basic attributes of the 'morally educated' person is that sort of insight into and involvement with others' feelings in such a way as to allow *their* interests, the way they see a situation, to weigh with him in the making of moral judgements, then literature provides us with an extremely valuable exercise of this capacity. This is the truth implicit in Shelley's claim in his *Defence of Poetry* cited earlier.

For literature does not simply involve us with characters sufficiently like ourselves, in certain situations; it also projects a particular conception of human character itself. You will get very different views of the capacities of human beings for good and evil by reading Dickens, George Eliot, Dostoevsky, D. H. Lawrence, Ivy Compton-Burnett, Samuel Beckett and Iris Murdoch, or even Kingsley Amis and Ian Fleming. Such moral conceptions are primary components in the explicit or implicit ideologies of a work. Literature thus populates our imagined universe with a great diversity of human characters, and with different types of moral agent, different estimates of what the possibilities for moral action of human beings are. This knowledge increases our own freedom by also giving us knowledge of its very limitations.[6]

Thus, to take an exaggerated example, in *Antony and Cleopatra* Shakespeare is concerned to show us how individual human characters can affect the course of grand historical events, since he accepts from Plutarch and elsewhere that history can be written from this point of of view. (Compare this to the obverse in Tolstoy.) His protagonists, by virtue of their wealth, their military and their political power, are endowed with an almost superhuman freedom of action, and their conception of the greatness of their own characters corresponds to this. Cleopatra says of Antony:

> in his livery
> Walked crowns and crownets, realms and islands were
> As plates dropped from his pocket   (V.ii. 90–92)

Some critics, probably with works like *Antony and Cleopatra* in mind, have wanted to maintain that our emotional involvement with, and understanding of a particular literary type, the Hero, has very profound psychological effects. (See the quotation given from Graham Hough earlier.) Thus Antony and Lancelot, Ulysses, Holden Caulfield, or John Wayne in a western or war film, let alone Hamlet or Lear or Macbeth in more complicated ways, are all thought to satisfy deep psychological needs, 'power craving', the need for a leader in relation to a particular community, and so on.[7] Although the truth of these sorts of view is as uncertain as the types of Freudian or Jungian depth psychology upon which they are based, they would certainly tend to demonstrate a morally significant response which is distinctive of literature.

These two rather general points about emotional response and about conceptions of character can, I think, be given more force by being attached to our first line of argument, which tried

---

6. For some philosophical underpinning of this remark, see, for example, Stuart Hampshire, *Thought and Action*, Chatto & Windus, 1959, Chapter III.

7. See also T. R. Henn, *The Harvest of Tragedy*, Methuen, 1966, pp. 83ff, and Maud Bodkin, *Archetypal Patterns in Pottery*, Oxford University Press, 1963, Chapter V. Some such assumption seems to underpin Northrop Frye's initial classification of heroes in his *Anatomy of Criticism*, Princeton, 1957. The hero is of similar importance to Angus Fletcher in his *Allegory: the theory of a symbolic mode*, Ithaca, New York, 1964, especially Chapter I.

to show that literature deals with moral problems distinctively and well.

In what follows, then, I wish to confine myself to the discussion of tragedy, as one of the more difficult cases of the relationship between literature, moral beliefs, and effects. I shall not be attempting to *define* tragedy, although I shall try to confine myself to what I think is tragic and not something else (for example, melodramatic or merely serious); and I shall not necessarily be concerned with the most important things about tragedy.

A moral interpretation of tragedy is almost forced upon us by the very heterogeneity of the language which has traditionally been found necessary to discuss it. It seems that in writing about *Oedipus, Lear,* and so on, we cannot as literary critics limit ourselves to the concepts of technical analysis (plot, story, probability, and so on). We have already apparently, to make decisions, to take up general ideological and moral commitments.

Thus Professor Henn, for example, clearly considers that such matters as evil and suffering in tragedy cannot be correctly understood (interpreted) except from the Christian point of view, which provides for him the best interpretation of tragic events.[8] His belief in redemption through suffering makes him ask of tragedy how it measures up to the Christian solution of the problem (if there is one). I believe, however, that the Christian view of divine providence, retribution for sin, compensation in the hereafter for suffering, goes directly against such tragic facts as I shall refer to below, and cannot be a true interpretation of the evidence provided by the literary tradition as a whole, let alone by certain individual works. However, even if we reject revealed religion as a primary source of insight into tragedy, then the nagging residua of the *problems* of religion (in Chekhov's sense), of 'man's sinful nature', and his accountability to 'a higher power', his responsibility and his freedom, and his chances of self-justification by dying if he has to die, still remain and are to be found in the tradition of tragedy.

It is from this point of view that I take issue also with George Steiner, who in *The Death of Tragedy* sees metaphysical commitments as making the actual writing of tragedy imposs-

---

8. T. R. Henn, *op. cit.*, Chapter VII, and sections iv and v in his concluding chapter.

ible. ('The metaphysics of Christianity and Marxism are anti-tragic. That in essence is the dilemma of modern tragedy'.[9]) Now if metaphysics of this type *were* essentially involved in tragedy, then the redemptive metaphysics of Christianity and Marxism would indeed make tragedy in some sense impossible. But metaphysics of these types are *not* essentially so involved, and so Steiner's proposition is false, largely because it makes a false empirical assumption. For I believe with Stuart Hampshire that 'the sources of the philosophical ideas that make an action, represented or real, a tragic action, are primarily the subject matter of individual psychology, if not of philosophy', and not of metaphysical ideologies.[10] Our involvement with such individual psychology, and its philosophical implications, forms the major part of the moral effect of literature. But having taken up these commitments, I had better try to make them good.

How then does tragedy investigate human psychology and action in a morally distinctive way? It does so in one very important way, it seems to me, by investigating and testing the concept of *responsibility*. (Of course, the classic example of this is the *Oedipus Rex*: how far is Oedipus responsible for actions taken in ignorance? Why does he accept guilt? Is he hubristic in failing to accept the prophecy made in his youth; or in his anger with Tiresias? But I do not wish this play to have the force of a paradigm in my argument; it has had a good run since Aristotle.) I shall argue that it is disasters for which human agents can properly be called responsible (and not the all-powerful gods, or natural processes including all types of disease) that are tragic in the full sense. I thus follow A. C. Bradley, who says that 'no mere suffering or misfortune, no suffering that does not spring in great part from human agency, and in some degree from the agency of the sufferer, is tragic'.[11]

Yet to establish this point we have first to meet the objection that accidental disasters may also be tragic. Thus Raymond Williams would extend the role of human responsibility to include what appear to be accidents—a mining disaster, a burned out family, a broken career or a smash on the road, or even wars, by placing them, so far as I understand him, within a

9. George Steiner, *The Death of Tragedy*, Faber, 1961, p. 324.

10. Stuart Hampshire, in *The Modern Writer and Other Essays*, Chatto & Windus, 1969, p. 186.

11. A. C. Bradley, *Oxford Lectures on Poetry*, Macmillan, 1909, 1958, p. 81.

wider context of social responsibility which we all share as members of a society which allows these things to happen.[12] Thus if we look far enough, what seems to be (merely) accidental suffering has an 'ethical content' and can be connected with 'general meanings'. I would agree, but point out that such complexes of events very rarely manage to become part of the content of tragedies such as we have them.

In the face of these difficulties we can appeal to Robert Heilman, who has produced arguments to show that we need to have additional critical categories such as the drama of disaster, or melodrama, in order to make this distinction concerning the limits of human responsibility. Whereas the drama of disaster goes beyond the range of human responsibility—'fatal accidents, mortal illnesses that strike (we think) before their time, the destructive blows of a nature not yet quite tamed, and all the murderous violence that comes directly or by ricochet, from the envious, the hostile, the mad'—melodrama stays within this range.[13] Tragedy occupies the problematic ground in between. It will be seen immediately from Heilman and Williams, though, that the fixing of such limits is as much a philosophical question as one of literary criticism.

Perhaps it is worth introducing at this point two examples within the literary tradition which seem to me to stand at these two extremes—one of strictly personal responsibility, and the other of a more general social or metaphysical responsibility—and then to contrast these with the melodramatic.

From the start of *Antony and Cleopatra* Antony is both judged:

> this dotage of our general's
> O'erflows the measure: (I.i.1–2)

and judges himself:

> These strong Egyptian fetters I must break,
> Or lose myself in dotage. (I.ii.113–14)

And he ultimately chooses wrongly, not perhaps in terms of some 'higher ethic', as the apotheosis of the lovers at the end might suggest, but certainly in terms of the human action of the play, when he submerges his political clearsightedness in

---

12. Raymond Williams, *Modern Tragedy*, Chatto & Windus, 1966, pp. 46ff.

13. Robert Heilman, *Tragedy and Melodrama*, Seattle and London, 1968, Chapters II and III especially. The quotation is from p. 47.

romantic love, 'claps on his seawing, and like a doting mallard' deserts his men in battle. Shakespeare's very conception of the historical process and of his protagonists involves a direct relationship between personal morality, individual action and (disastrously in this case) political consequences. In view of this, some critics may well feel as I do that *Antony and Cleopatra* is nearer the melodramatic than the tragic end of the scale.

Kafka's *Trial*, however, is much more complicated. We have what might be called the tragedy of the victim:

> Someone must have been telling lies about Joseph K, for without having done anything wrong, he was arrested one fine morning.

So runs the opening sentence. We begin with a man who has been held responsible for a crime which he did not commit. Yet the enigma of the book for many readers lies in deciding just what Joseph K is, or believes himself, responsible for, which may be a mere sense of guilt, and in speculating on the nature of that 'Law' by which he is, or is not, judged. For we see too that Kafka has set in acute form a problem for those who (like Henn) believe that tragedy leads us to speculate upon the nature of laws, divine, natural and human:[14]

> 'I don't know this law', said K. 'All the worse for you,' replied the warder. 'And it probably exists nowhere but in your head', said K.

This and many other details show that K is involved in a totalitarian bureaucratic nightmare. We are hardly surprised that when K inspects the Law book he finds that it contains nothing but obscene pictures and stories. The force of the book from the point of view of responsibility is that the operation of the Law upon Joseph K is totally disreputable by the standards which *we* bring to the book (unless we accept that K has some kind of Absurdist metaphysical guilt). For as the Advocate explains, the accused doesn't know the charge against him, the defence proceeds by hearsay and bribery, and in every case 'Progress has always been made but the nature of the progress could never be divulged'.[15] This *tests* our notions of

---

14. Henn, *op. cit.*, p. 283.
15. Franz Kafka, *The Trial*, tr. Willa and Edwin Muir, Harmondsworth, 1953, pp. 126ff. The quotation is from p. 138; the preceding one from p. 13.

the ascription of responsibility within society. (It need hardly be pointed out that Kafka's presentation of the 'law' here is far from being a mere fantasy.)

Now Heilman and I would no doubt be in dispute as to whether *The Trial* is tragedy or melodrama: the passivity of the victim here seems to leave us with a tale of two opposing forces—the individual and society. But my point is that a decision about this (and an essential interpretative decision about the meaning of the book) does indeed turn upon the question of K's responsibility; and, if one wishes to remove oneself as far as Williams, of our responsibility for societies of the type which destroys K. (Societies which we also see portrayed in Dürrenmatt's *The Visit*, Max Frisch's *Andorra* and Solzhenitsyn's *Cancer Ward*, though from different perspectives.)

In the melodramatic play or novel (or poem, like *Absalom and Achitophel*) the lines of opposition are clear cut and demand a solution. Heilman remarks that a drama like Dürrenmatt's *The Visit* works like 'a shocking cartoon, a knockout critique in grotesque images', and he comments:

> When it functions in this way, the literature of disaster shows its affinity with satire, which by its nature keeps us decisively outside of the reality that it represents ... The foible or vice is always over there outside us, in others; it is not conceivably within us. This, it need hardly be said, is a long way from tragedy.[16]

But the very nature of the vice 'outside us', in *The Trial* is far from clear; the nature of the Law itself is in question, and we are deeply involved with K, to the point of sharing his feelings of guilt. This inward and outward questioning is a mark of tragedy and its chief moral effect. Thus, as Heilman goes on to argue:

> Melodrama is the realm of social action, public action, action within the world; tragedy is the realm of private action, action within the soul. Melodrama is concerned with making right prevail in the world and between persons, or with observing that it does not prevail; tragedy with the problem of right in the self.[17]

---

16. Heilman, *op. cit.*, p. 46.
17. Heilman, *op. cit.*, p. 97.

The formal progress of the action is of course crucial here, for the protagonist's responsibility is located within that elaborate autonomic sequence of cause and effect centring on hamartia, hubris, peripeteia, anagnorisis of the nature of the thing done and of the self as doer, and catastrophe, which Aristotle was the first to attempt to specify. The tragic protagonist has to take some decision or make some act of will that will initiate such a sequence. Suppose only that Hamlet stops worrying about his domestic situation or that Orestes concludes that Agamemnon should have been murdered, or that Cordelia decides to humour an angry old man. Such responses to dilemmatic conflicts just do not occur in tragedy. Hamlet has his recognition scene at the very beginning of his play (even if he does doubt the Ghost). He is in no way responsible for the situation revealed to him, and yet he is set on his course of action by obeying an imperative from his father, and in resisting his impulse to retreat from the situation thereafter. Yet all these protagonists end badly (as Macbeth does).

Thus that element which seems to me to be of prime moral importance within the Aristotelian framework is a genuinely dilemmatic conflict or tension centred on or within the main protagonist, involving responsibility. The tragic hero may have to confront the gods, or society, with their imperatives and their justice, or undergo the malign influence of the slowly revealed past upon the present, or be prey to terrible internal strife. The hero has to reconcile these external demands with his own projects. Mere confrontation, as in *Doctor Faustus*, produces melodrama, until the pangs of conscience at the end produce tragedy. Similarly, what makes Macbeth into a tragic hero rather than melodramatic villain is his conscience and his imagination.

It might be thought, in the context of responsibility we have so far argued for, that by the end of the tragic work we are brought to witness a kind of punishment. (Indeed the whole of *The Trial* may be thought of in this way.) I realize that in talking about the end result of such actions as 'punishment' I am extending the legalistic sense of the term considerably. It is a concept that may seem more applicable to *Volpone* than to *King Lear*. But I find the contrast between our judicial concept of punishment, which depends at the moment upon contested concepts of retribution and reform, and the disaster of tragic events particularly illuminating. This is especially so if we wish to understand the relationship between the main part of the tragic action and its ending (in that atmosphere of necessity, which is so easily associated with the judicial process). There may well be a case for asking whether the tragic hero or heroine is justly or unjustly punished for his actions.

It thus seems to me not at all surprising that the great disputes about tragedy in the eighteenth century, when the older metaphysical frameworks were collapsing, centred on the concept of 'poetic justice'. Discussions of tragedy in the modern period, especially those aroused by Hegel's notion of a 'split in the ethical substance' or of two competing goods seeking reconciliation in some higher dialectic, have really addressed themselves to the same problem. Although neither the eighteenth-century solution (showing suffering as a consequence of error and happiness as the consequence of virtue), nor the Hegelian one (making a reconciliation of the conflict in the interests of society or the Absolute at the cost of destroying the individual) are entirely satisfactory, they do point to one of the ways in which tragedy has a very great strength. For it is when the catastrophe arouses some such sense of justice that it involves us (as Henn points out) in 'the ambivalent attitudes of recognition, participation in and conscious rejection of, major moral values'.[18] These values can then often be seen in relation to various ideological frameworks of order.

Thus *Antony and Cleopatra* is indeed centred upon a conflict or dilemma very much of a Hegelian cast and, if we took a particular view of the legitimacy of Roman power in Octavius Caesar, we would even have a clearly Hegelian solution on the political level. But the real force of the catastrophe lies within the psychology of the protagonists. They both deliberately choose ritual deaths. These deaths are not entirely those of sadness, waste and futility as in *Lear*, but assert the contingent human value of personal greatness and romantic love against the background of an irreconcilable political conflict. For:

> The soul and body rive not more in parting
> Than greatness going off.   (IV.xiii.5–6)

---

18. Henn, *op. cit.*, p. 91.

The tragedy is one of a renunciation whose force derives from the protagonist's heroic stature:

> The soldier's pole is fall'n: young boys and girls
> Are level now with men; the odds is gone,
> And there is nothing left remarkable
> Beneath the visiting moon. (IV.xv.65–8)

And the imagery of the play, but not the facts of their last hours—Antony's botched attempt at suicide, Cleopatra's last attempt to trick Caesar—deceive us into believing that we are witnessing a carefully prepared apotheosis:

> Where souls do couch on flowers, we'll hand in hand,
> And with our sprightly port make the ghosts gaze. (V.xiv.51–2)

Thus Cleopatra says:

> I am fire, and air: my other elements
> I give to baser life. (V.ii.288–9)

And for Antony the values of love also become a very part of the act of dying:

> I will be
> A bridegroom in my death, and run into't
> As to a lover's bed. (IV.xiv.99–101)

Cleopatra too achieves an extraordinary metamorphosis, from 'serpent of old Nile', one who is 'with Phoebus' amorous pinches black', into the role of mother:

> Peace, peace,
> Dost thou not see my baby at my breast,
> That sucks the nurse asleep? (V.ii.307–9)

Antony and Cleopatra supports, I think, those who say that death in tragedy can have a redemptive function and thus be in some sense retributive: the guilty protagonists rise above the rights and wrongs of the action, and make their deaths an affirmation of some value which we accept as transcending it.

I realize that in concentrating on responsibility, I may well have left out the most important thing about tragedy; though I think that responsibility may well be the most important element in the relationship between tragedy and moral beliefs. I realize also that tragedy grossly extends our usual concept of responsibility, if we are not willing to accept the heroic ideal of Sartre and Camus. For I do not see how we can call the disastrous consequences of human actions *tragic*, if those actions were not in some sense responsibly undertaken and intended. For it is only in these circumstances that the death or punishment which is the tragic hero's fate can make any sense. Otherwise the ending of tragedy is arbitrary and destructive, pathetic perhaps, even outrageous, but not tragic. Certainly the punishment may be excessive; is the little world of Denmark so rotten that the deaths of Polonius, Ophelia, Laertes, as well as of Gertrude and Claudius are justified? For Hamlet's revenge certainly exceeds his brief, which was only directed against Claudius. Perhaps the very excess of the tragic catastrophe here throws into relief the values for which human beings may have to (be willing to) die. For, as I hope I have shown, it is not just the 'working out' in tragedy that is of importance, or even perhaps of ultimate importance, from the point of view of moral effect. It is the individual values held to by human beings in the face of disaster and failure that count. A central theme of tragedy would thus be, as Antony Quinton asserts,

> the contingency of value. Whatever is of value in the world [the tragic vision asserts] is due to man. Not merely in the sense that without human purposes and satisfactions nothing would be of value at all, though this may be presupposed, but rather that the achievement and maintenance of value in the world can only be brought about by the efforts of man.[19]

Thus in saying that tragedy is about responsibility and defeat or apparent defeat, I could have said, tragedy is about our freedom, as expressed through the characters of K, Antony, Lear,

19. Anthony Quinton, 'Tragedy', *Proceedings of the Aristoteleian Society*, 1957, p. 162. On this see also R. M. Hare, *Freedom and Reason*, Oxford University Press, 1963, pp. 167ff.; William Frankena, 'Recent Conceptions of Morality' in H. Castaneda and Nakhnikian, eds., *Morality and the Language of Conduct*, Detroit, 1965, which discusses the opposition between formal and individualistic conceptions of morality, and material and social definitions of it. See also W. D. Falk, 'Morality, self and others' in the same volume, and Alexander Solzhenitsyn, defending himself at a session of he Secretariat of the Union of Soviet Writers, 22 September 1967, in Leopold Labedz, ed., *Solzhenitsyn: a documentary record*, Harmondsworth, 1970, p. 147.

to create our own values, and to hold them with, or against, any larger framework of belief.

If my argument is to any degree valid, then we can look to tragic literature to gain a much more complex and penetrating picture of the world than we possess in our ordinary moments. It can test our unreflective philosophical, moral and even political assumptions. In the greatest cases (and I include tragic novels, like *Karamazov, Tess of the D'Urbervilles, Anna Karenina, Nostromo, L'Etranger*, and *The Heart of the Matter*) it tests the most basic elements in our philosophic and moral thinking.

Further Reading

For further reading, the reader is referred to the works cited in the footnotes.

Marxist Literary Criticism

TERRY EAGLETON

There is a sense in which no Marxist criticism worthy of the name can see itself merely as 'an approach' to literary texts, any more than Marxism as such views itself as merely one interpretation of history among many. Marxism claims to provide a scientific theory of social formations together with the practice of transforming them; and that claim entails the proposition that, until such a revolutionary transformation has taken place, its own analysis cannot be outstripped by another. However, it can be, and is, continually enriched and elaborated by other versions of history; but since it claims to expose the *fundamental* contradictions of contemporary societies, it must regard itself as an horizon which can be ignored but not, as yet, historically transcended.

The same standpoint applies to that specialized sector of Marxist theory which we know as Marxist aesthetics. Marxist aesthetics must discourteously refuse to occupy its modest niche within the expansive range of 'approaches' to art. It has learnt too often the emasculating perils of such cheerful accommodation. To be sure, Marxist aesthetics can learn much from bourgeois criticism. But it stands or falls by its claim to illuminate and surpass the ideological limits of bourgeois criticism, 'placing' and challenging the latter's overt or unconscious assumptions. The intention of Marxist criticism is not to dismiss the insights of, say, stylistic, psychoanalytic or even straight empiricist criticism, but to establish a hierarchy among these alternative methods, and in so doing to constitute itself as that hierarchy's determining 'base'.

Marxist criticism, then, has little in common with what is conventionally known as the 'social' approach to literature. The assumptions embodied in that approach are fairly familiar: there are some texts, or levels of texts, which contain historical or sociological material, and we call in the 'social' critic to attend to these in the same way as we refer segments of Kafka to the theologian and slices of Thomas Mann to the scientist.

According to this view, the sociologist has his uses, just as the metaphysician does, when it comes to a poet such as Blake; and the critic proper, unlabelled and unspecialized, may raid their professional offerings to underpin or eke out his own merely 'human' account. For the rest of his time, the sociological critic behaves like a kind of distant cousin of the traditional literary scholar: whereas the latter busies himself with the literary-historical outworks of the imaginative text, the former provides empirical information about the means of literary production, distribution and exchange. In other words, it is assumed that the distinctly social critic unpacks his professional tool-kit only when such a writer as Mrs Gaskell appears in his critical sights, but closes it up again when a Christina Rossetti comes into view.

It is clear enough, I suppose, that no self-respecting Marxist criticism can have truck with such a conveniently withered meaning of the 'social'. The aim of Marxist criticism, on the contrary, is to expose the ideological tendentiousness implicit in that familiar narrowing of the social to a question of cotton-mills and bread-riots. For while only some literature is 'social problem' literature, all imaginative production is social pro-duction. The social is never merely one particular term to be casually equalized with others, say, mythological, sexual, per-sonal, or political. It is the matrix within which all other terms are fleshed and shaped. Of course, there are trans-historical continuities: there is sexual passion in the plays of Webster as there is in the poetry of Yeats. But to say that is to say almost nothing, critically speaking. How that passion is catalyzed and articulated, what issues it engages, what dramas it fashions: these questions lead us directly to consider the changing forms of historical consciousness. And it is a curiously narrow notion of history which would ask of a literary gesture whether it is 'historical' or 'timeless', as though history were only the history of an author's immediate society, and all else a matter of eternal recurrence.

If the relation between literature and society is to be more than a simple-minded one-to-one correlation of 'literary' and 'social' detail, this relation must surely involve some concept of structure. The most dominant European tradition of Marxist criticism—the neo-Hegelian lineage of George Lukács, Theodor Adorno, Herbert Marcuse, Lucien Goldmann,

Jean-Paul Sartre, and Raymond Williams[1]—has indeed been preoccupied with just that notion. Marxist criticism has tried to discover some *synchrony* of structure whereby we are able to decipher the outline of an informing structure of social consciousness in the aesthetic forms of the text itself, simultaneously grasping that this shaping social consciousness results from an organization of historical forces. One achievement of this critical enterprise is to liberate criticism from the magic spell of that liberal dogma which sees art as organizing the 'chaos' of reality, as imposing form on the formless, order on the amorphous. Instead we are led to ask what kind of society, what kind of ideology is it which *sees* reality as 'chaotic'? In the neo-Hegelian tradition, the relation between literature and society appears rather in the form of a set of complex connections between a 'first order' structure, that is, history itself, and a 'second order' structure, that is, the literature that history produces. The problem for criticism, then, becomes one of how each 'level' or 'order' of the structural model referred to above (text, social consciousness, history) is mediated and transformed into the others.

One immediate gain of the neo-Hegelian critical method is that it promises to root literature in social conditions without reducing it to them. As such it confidently outflanks those modes of vulgar Marxist criticism, rampant in Britain in the 1930s, which threatened to shrivel literary texts to the mere passive reflexes of a determining economic base. This was never the method of Marx and Engels themselves, or of the great tradition of Marxist criticism which followed them. Marx himself had a continuing, life-long engagement with the question of literary production: right from his own early ventures in writing poetry, tragedy and a comic novel, to the aesthetic implications of some of the categories he uses in *Das Kapital*, literature and art were for Marx phenomena of profound, sometimes paradigmatic significance. Art is a controversial issue in his early relations with Hegel and the young Hegelians; it figures prominently in his analysis of ancient societies, and in the form of an onslaught on Romanticism enters into his critique of the reactionary German ruling class of his own day. Its influence can be detected in some of his most central concepts—fetishism,

---

1. I include Williams because his work clearly belongs with this tradition, although he is not a Marxist.

production, ideology, sensuousness, universality, abstraction. In Marx's early writings art incarnates a complex, many-sided sensuous richness which a philistine capitalism needs to quantify and negate. Marx and Engels never speak of art and literature as though they were merely the reflex of a particular stage of development of a mode of production; on the contrary, they see art as a specific illustration of the unevenness and indirection with which the superstructure of a society's consciousness forms a complex whole with its material base. Engels once remarked that art was the most mediated of all social phenomena, and that insight is elaborated in the work of critics like Mehring, Plekhanov and Trotsky. Trotsky's *Literature and Revolution* launches an uncompromising critique of contemporary bourgeois art-forms, but is discriminatingly responsive to the qualities they can offer to a developed socialist culture.

The problem of mediations between literature and society, then, is implicit in the work of Marx and Engels themselves. Like any element of the superstructure (which is conceived of by Marx as those institutions and forms of consciousness which grow up on the basis of a determining economic system), literature has its own relative autonomy, its own internally evolving forms and histories. But its final determinants are to be found in the complex interactions literature sets up with other superstructural elements and with the economic base. The neo-Hegelian critical tradition, cued by the absence of any fully developed theory of superstructures in Marx's own writings, then tries to specify more precisely what those interactions might be. It grasps the relations between literature and history, not primarily at the level of an ideological content abstractable from the texts themselves (such as we encounter in 'background' studies), but at the level of literary *form*. Marxist criticism maintains against bourgeois formalism that 'form' is in the last instance produced by 'content', but that that determination is not to be mechanistically interpreted. The 'content' of an historical society has for Marxism an internal logic or structure of its own; and the project of neo-Hegelian Marxist criticism is to grasp the dialectics whereby that historical logic can be 'read' in the formal structures of literary works.

A major example is the concept of realism as developed by Georg Lukács, the Hungarian Marxist critic. For Lukács, realism signifies not mere representativeness but a work rich in a complex, rounded and integrated totality of relations between man, nature and history, relations which, by fleshing out the 'typical' trends and forces of an epoch, inform each concrete particular with the power of the universal. Realism, in this deeper sense of the *totality* of relations in social life, contrasts with that bourgeois modernism which can display only abstract symbolic cyphers of experience stripped of their social reality, adrift in a directionless flow of merely interior time. The great realists such as Balzac and Scott, Lukács argues, arise at historical conjunctures where the fragmenting, abstracting and dehumanizing forces of industrial capitalism are relatively undeveloped, so that those forces can still be 'totalized', or viewed in the larger perspective of history, as well as in the full and immediate context of society at a particular time, and evaluated from the standpoint of some traditional idea of human wholeness. Realism, then, is inseparably a descriptive and evaluative term: the more effectively the work reproduces the 'typical' components of its history, fashioning these into an 'intensive totality' which microcosmically reflects the society in which it is rooted, the richer, fuller, more unified and universally significant it becomes.

Lucien Goldmann, the Rumanian Marxist critic, follows Lukács in discovering a nexus between literature and history at the level of form. Goldmann, too, is concerned with the problem of how a specific historical structure is transformed by literary production to emerge in its turn as the internal structure of a text; and the mediatory concept he uses here is that of 'world view'. Goldmann analyses the 'world view' of a work for the degree to which it expresses the mental structures of the social group or class to which the writer belongs; and the more a work approximates to a full, coherent articulation of that class's world view, the greater its validity for Goldmann as an aesthetic product. His critical method is to move constantly between the internal forms of a text and its historically surrounding structure of consciousness; and in this his method finds an echo in Raymond Williams's concept of a 'structure of feeling'. For Williams, 'structure of feeling' signifies the elusive complex of lived values which we find in the world of the work, but which links it outwards to the significantly patterned sensibility of the work's historical era. And for Williams as for Goldmann—although a good deal less directly—that structure of historical experience has its moment of genesis in the organization of 'real' historical forces.

Permanently valuable though much in the neo-Hegelian tradition is, that heritage is nonetheless constricted by severe limits. Many of its flaws, and indeed blind spots, arise from its failure to prise itself wholly free from the assumptions of bourgeois criticism, so that at its worst it reproduces the dominant modes of that criticism with a saving tinge of materialism. Like bourgeois criticism, it tends to view the literary product primarily as an object, an object to be obliquely related to a history which stands over against it. As such, and especially in the case of Lukács, there is something peculiarly static and abstracting about neo-Hegelian aesthetics. Like bourgeois criticism, too, the neo-Hegelian tradition moves almost entirely in the privileged domain of *consciousness*, shut off from a recognition of literature as a concrete social practice with a material 'infrastructure'.

Both Lukács and Goldmann, moreover, tend to make a fetish of 'totality', celebrating the harmonious and the integrated; and this, at its worst, merely transposes to a different key the bourgeois mythology of the 'organic' artefact. Goldmann's models of 'levels'—text, world view, history—suffers considerably from this excessive pursuit of symmetry. His emphasis falls heavily on the transparency with which each 'level' shines, as it were, through the others, rather than on the dialectical, refracted, asymmetrical relations between literary production and other facets of the social formation. For Goldmann the text is 'expressive' of class-consciousness, and class-consciousness 'expressive' of historical forces. But such a model, apart from leaving too many 'levels' out of account, cannot fully answer to the intransigent complexity of the issues at stake. Lukács's rather different preoccupation with symmetry reveals itself in his nostalgic, backward-looking, idealist notion of 'wholeness', which he sees as some primordial human integration rudely shattered by the productive forces and the philistine materialism of capitalist society. Hence his stiff-necked, classicist contempt for modernist experiment, which he can see only as undifferentiated bourgeois decadence. Strange, though it may seem, Lukács's aggressive closedness to modernism, his hunger for organic unity, his projection of one historically particular *genre* of fiction into an archetype of the universally valid, his relative casualness about the close textual analysis of novels, give his work more than a superficial resemblance to that of F. R. Leavis.

There is, however, another way of considering the structural relations between literature and history within the modern Marxist tradition. This is a form of Marxist criticism which sees literary form as a consequence of the technical and ideological conditions of the work's production. This critical mode, closely associated with the names of Bertholt Brecht and Walter Benjamin, inaugurates a radical break with that whole Romantic discourse about art which turns on the idea of the artist as 'creator' and his artefact as 'imaginative creation'. For this alternative Marxist tradition, art is primarily production and practice.

Benjamin, unlike Lukacs and Goldmann, asks first about the artist's historical place *within* the means of production rather than the ideological relation of his product to those means. For Brecht, the play isn't a self-sealed object proffered for consumption, but an open-ended, continuously transformable practice in whose making and re-making an audience actively collaborates. Just as developments in the forces of social production generate fresh social relations, so practical innovations in the material infrastructures of artistic production result in new artistic forms which embody a changed set of social relations between the producer and his audience. Literature, like any other social practice, employs determinate means of production to transform a determinate 'raw material' into a specific product; and a systematic analysis of the mechanisms of this practice in particular literary works is an important task for Marxist criticism.

What needs to be examined also is the relations between the material and ideological conditions of a work's production. If Brecht, Benjamin and their successors focus primarily on the first, the work of some recent European Marxist critics influenced by Louis Althusser has concentrated its attention chiefly on the second. The most suggestive of these critics is Pierre Macherey, whose work[2] deserves to be better known in Britain than it is. Macherey's aim is to establish a scientific critical knowledge. He rejects the various forms of empiricist criticism, which either reduplicate a text in different

---

2. *Pour une Théorie de la Production Littéraire*, Paris, 1966.

language, 'correct' it according to a normative model of what it should be, or try to elicit some secret structure immanent in it. Instead, he sees the true domain of criticism as an explanation of the *conditions of the work's possibility*, conditions which for Macherey are not primarily material, but which inscribe themselves within the text as the limits of what the text can say.

Every text is produced from within an ideological world which circumscribes its vision; and in trying to register reality faithfully, the text will press up against the frontiers of what can be said, thus exposing those ideological frontiers and allowing the critic to identify them. It is these limits which Macherey has in mind when he speaks of the conditions of a work's possibility, and it is in giving some systematic account of how the text, given these limits, cannot but speak as it does, that for Macherey the critic's true task lies. A text, in saying one thing, will reveal other possibilities, other statements and insights, which it is ideologically prohibited from realizing; and the absence of those other possibilities will create tensions, disparities, contradictions in what the text actually does say.

It is, in other words, the *absences*, the silences and hiatuses, in a text which for Macherey tie it most closely to the history from which it is produced; and this notion involves a radical de-mystification of the Romantic myth of the literary work as organic, integrated, self-complete. For Macherey, the text is, on the contrary, always unachieved, 'decentred', irregular, dispersed, constituted by a conflict and contradiction of meanings, and a scientific criticism will seek for the principle of this diversity. Macherey's scientific criticism installs itself in the very 'incompleteness' of the text—in what the text does not and cannot say—and theorizes this incompleteness. Its task is to identify the 'absences' around which the text's complexity of meaning knots itself. George Eliot's novels, to select one example, reveal a structural conflict between Romantic individualism—'the free spirit'—and the need to conform submissively to a totality 'higher' than the individual self; but what the novels cannot speak of is that this conflict is itself an insurmountable contradiction in bourgeois ideology which only a revolutionary social change could possibly abolish. Forbidden to recognize this truth, the novels are forced into mythical devices, structural dissonances, unwarrantable interventions; it is in this sense that their 'absences' produce a conflict of meaning. The author is not the 'creator' but the *worker* of his text, producing it by certain determinant techniques in certain determinate conditions; and those conditions reveal themselves in the 'not-said' of the work, in the disparity between what it would like, and what it is obliged, to speak of.

Macherey rejects the structuralist hypothesis that explaining a text consists in reducing its surface complexity to a concealed 'message', finding in this duality between surface and depths, appearance and reality, exterior and interior, merely a fresh version of what he terms 'theological' or 'Platonic' criticism. For him, nothing in a text is concealed, all lies open to view. It is in the unfolding of the work's irreducible complexity, not in the ghostly presence of some single secret essence, that the text has its significance.

Marxist criticism has been traditionally vulnerable to the charge that its conceptual ambitiousness squeezes out a concern for what one might call a work's most immediate presence— its form and style, imagery and syntax, diction and rhythm. The work of Lukacs, and to some extent of Goldmann, is certainly susceptible of such an accusation, as are the writings of Christopher Caudwell, Ernst Fischer and Raymond Williams. But the same cannot be said of the literary work of Marx, Lenin, Trotsky, Walter Benjamin, Theodor Adorno. What Marxist criticism wants to enforce above all is that the dichotomy between an analysis of the social determinants of literature on the one hand, and a concern for the 'words on the page' on the other, is itself an *ideological* dichotomy, the product of a society which has good reasons for dismissing concern with the historical determinants of literary production as emptily abstract. The purpose of Marxist criticism, like any literary analysis, is to possess the work more deeply. We are not attending to the 'words on the page' if we fail to grasp them as the cryptic but revelatory signs of a real history. That grasp is, naturally, an *evaluative* one. Marxist *criticism* aims for more than a merely descriptive account of the work's historical mode of existence. The vulgar Marxist case that 'aesthetically valuable' equals 'politically progressive' was never, of course, the conclusion of Marx and Engels themselves. A work's sensitivity to the 'typical', developing dynamics of its history is indeed a major constituent of its aesthetic worth, but, as Marx pointed out in the case of Balzac, that sensitivity may be locked in productive conflict with the conscious ideological stance of the author. It may well be that most of the agreed masters of twentieth-century literature are all right-wing conservatives or (sporadically) fascists, but that contradiction can be resolved only by a dialectical criticism. What Yeats, Eliot, Pound and Lawrence had in common was their fierce opposition to bourgeois society, to the priorities of liberal-democratic industrial capitalism. In that situation, given the historically determined absence of a revolutionary critique, it was radical conservatism which filled the vacuum, summoning resources which transcended the superannuated liberal bourgeois heritage of a Virginia Woolf or an E. M. Forster.

While that inherited liberal humanist ideology continues to sustain most conventional literary criticism in the West, it is currently showing symptoms of radical self-doubt. As the liberal-democratic centreground continues to crumble under the sharpening pressures of world capitalist crisis, the oblique, implicit, confident assumptions which underpin the civilized activity of criticism can no longer claim widespread intuitive endorsement. The hunt for 'long perspectives' is on, as literary criticism feels the pressing need for a more ambitious, totalizing framework to buttress its credibility. Myth, 'culture criticism', Structuralism, *genre*, theology, the history of ideas: these are some of the proposed alternatives to mere technocratic specialism or cultivated amateurism. What is urgently needed, however, is a truly dialectical criticism, conscious of its historical roots and relations, and so capable of interrogating the limits of other critical methods which substitute their own *synthetic* totalities (whether it be 'myth', '*genre*', the 'history of ideas') for the founding totality of history itself. It is the claim of Marxist criticism to provide such an analysis.

Further Reading

Henri Arvon, *Marxist Aesthetics* (Cornell), 1973.
Terry Eagleton, *Shakespeare and Society*, Chatto & Windus, 1967. *Exiles and Emigres*, Chatto & Windus, 1970.
G. Lukács, *The Historical Novel* (London, Merlin Press), 1962. *Studies in European Realism* (London, Hillway), 1950.
Fredric Jameson, *Marxism and Form* (Princeton), 1971.

Notes on Contributors

CHRISTOPHER BUTLER was born in 1940 and educated at Brentwood School and Brasenose College, Oxford. He was Senior Hulme Scholar at Brasenose College, then Research Lecturer at Christchurch, Oxford, where he is at present Student (i.e. Fellow) in English Literature. His publications include *Number Symbolism*, 1970, and (with Alastair Fowler) *Topics in Criticism*, 1971. He is currently at work on various themes in critical theory, and on a book on *Post-Modernism: the Arts since 1945*.

JONATHAN CULLER was born in the U.S.A. in 1944. He was educated at Harvard where he obtained his B.A., *summa cum laude*, in History and Literature in 1966. He then came to Oxford as a Rhodes Scholar where he obtained his B.Phil in Comparative Literature, and D.Phil. in Modern Languages. From 1969–74 he was Fellow and Director of Studies in Modern Languages at Selwyn College, Cambridge. He then returned to Oxford where he is now University Lecturer in French, and Fellow and Tutor of Brasenose College. In the Autumn of 1975 he was Visiting Professor of French and Comparative Literature at Yale. His publications include: *Flaubert: The Uses of Uncertainty*, 1974; *Structuralist Poetics: Structuralism, Linguistics and the Study of Literature*, 1975; and *Saussure* (Fontana Modern Masters Series), 1976.

TERRY EAGLETON was born in 1943 and educated at Trinity College, Cambridge. He was Fellow of Jesus College, Cambridge, between 1964 and 1969, and since then has been Tutorial Fellow of Wadham College, Oxford, and Lecturer in English in the University of Oxford. He is currently Visiting Professor at the University of California, San Diego. His publications include *Shakespeare and Society*, 1966; *Exiles and Emigrés*, 1970; *Myths of Power: A Marxist Study of the Brontës*, 1975; *Marxism and Literary Criticism*, in press.

LEON EDEL was born in the U.S.A. in 1907. He was educated at McGill University, Montreal, and the University of Paris where he obtained his Docteur-ès-Lettres in 1932. He served with the U.S. Army in Europe in the war and then returned to North America where he taught at numerous colleges and universities. Since 1970 he has been Citizens Professor of English in the University of Hawaii. He is a member of many learned societies, and amongst other distinctions was awarded the Pulitzer Prize for biography in 1963. His publications include *James Joyce: The Last Journey*, 1947; a five-volume biography, *The Life of Henry James*, 1953–1972; *The Psychological Novel*, 1955; *Literary Biography*, 1957; *Literary History and Literary Criticism*, 1965; and he has edited numerous volumes of Henry James's letters, plays and tales.

HILDA SCHIFF spent her childhood during the war and immediately afterwards roaming about Cornwall, Switzerland and the U.S.A. She was educated privately and at King's College, London, where she obtained her B.A. and M.A. research degree. She has been Tutor and Lecturer in English at Colleges and Extra-Mural Departments, and became a member of the Faculty of Education in the University of London in 1969. She is now a Tutor in the Open University. Her publications include poems, short stories and critical articles. At present she is working on a book on *The Idea of Science and the Growth of Criticism* which she began when she spent two years in Oxford between 1970 and 1972.

GEORGE STEINER was born in Paris in 1929 and educated in France, the U.S.A. and in England. He was a Rhodes Scholar at Balliol College, Oxford, where he obtained his D.Phil. He was a member of the Institute for Advanced Study in Princeton between 1956–58. In 1961 he became a Fellow of Churchill College, Cambridge. He has lectured widely throughout the world and is now Professor of Comparative Literature in the University of Geneva, as well as Extraordinary Fellow of Churchill College, Cambridge. He was President of the English Association in 1975. His publications include *Tolstoy or Dostoevsky*, 1958; *The Death of Tragedy*, 1960; *Anno Domini*, 1964 (a work of fiction); *Language ana Silence*, 1967; *Extraterritorial*, 1971; *In Bluebeard's Castle*, 1971; and *After Babel*, 1975.

RAYMOND WILLIAMS was born in 1921 and was educated at his local school at Pandy, at Abergavenny Grammar School, and at Trinity College, Cambridge. After the war he became Extra-Mural Tutor in the University of Oxford, and in 1961 became Fellow of Jesus College, Cambridge. He has been Professor of Drama in the University of Cambridge since 1974. He was Visiting Professor at Stanford University, U.S.A., in 1973. His publications include *Drama from Ibsen to Eliot*, 1952; *Drama in Performance*, 1954; *Culture and Society*, 1958; *The Long Revolution*, 1961; *Modern Tragedy*, 1966; *The English Novel from Dickens to Lawrence*, 1970; and *The Country and the City*, 1973. As well as criticism, he has written two novels: *Border Country*, 1960, and *Second Generation*, 1964. His latest publication is *Keywords, A Vocabulary of Culture and Society*, 1976.

The study of English as an accredited academic subject is a comparatively recent development. Early this century most educated people took it for granted that the understanding of one's own language and literature could be assumed. Today the position looks very different. Not only has English taken over much of the humanizing role formerly carried by Classics; it has also developed a great variety of different approaches.

It was in an attempt to take stock of these developments that the English Association commissioned the papers which make up this collection. The essays range widely over the present state of English in Britain, North America, and elsewhere, and some of the most significant specializations within the subject.

George Steiner's opening essay, *Why English?*, is a bold survey of the international nature of English today. Steiner shows how many of the most powerful currents in the developments of English language and literature now flow outside Britain. He argues for a strengthening of the content of English syllabuses in our schools and universities, bearing in mind that the study of language is the focal point of a consideration of our civilization.

Raymond Williams then explores in an altogether fresh and invigorating manner an area of concern to critics and social thinkers from Arnold to himself: the way in which we may study the place of literature in the society which produces it. The essay which follows, 'The Poetics of Biography', by the American biographer and critic, Leon Edel, is wittily cast in the form of a dialogue on the steps of the British Museum. Beneath the humour there emerges a trenchant critique of literary ideologies, and a serious claim for the central place of subjectivity in literary interpretation.